PEOPLE JESUS MET

Lon Solomon

Copyright © 2024 by Lon Solomon
First Paperback Edition

All rights reserved. No part of this publication may be reproduced, distributed, or transmitted in any form or by any means, including photocopying, recording, or other electronic or mechanical methods, without the prior written permission of the publisher, except in the case of brief quotations embodied in critical reviews and certain other noncommercial uses permitted by copyright law. For permission requests, write to the publisher, addressed

"Attention: Permissions Coordinator," at the address below. Some names, businesses, places, events, locales, incidents, and identifying details inside this book have been changed to protect the privacy of individuals.

Bible versions used:

King James Version (KJV). Public domain.

Holy Bible, New International Version®, NIV® Copyright © 1973, 1978, 1984, 2011 by Biblica, Inc.® Used by permission. All rights reserved worldwide.

New King James Version® (NKJV). Copyright © 1982 by Thomas Nelson. Used by permission. All rights reserved.

New American Standard Bible®, (NASB). Copyright © 1960, 1971, 1977, 1995, 2020 by The Lockman Foundation. All rights reserved.

The Holy Bible, English Standard Version. ESV® Text Edition: 2016. Copyright © 2001 by Crossway Bibles, a publishing ministry of Good News Publishers.

Published by Freiling Agency, LLC.

P.O. Box 1264
Warrenton, VA 20188

www.FreilingAgency.com

PB ISBN: 979-8-9897784-6-1
eBook ISBN: 979-8-9897784-7-8

Printed in the United States of America

Table of Contents

Foreword v
1 Mary and Joseph (God's Timing) 1
2 Satan (Scripture Memory) 15
3 The Paralytic (Mark 2:1–12) (Jesus' Authority to Forgive Sin) 31
4 Matthew (Following Jesus Correctly) 49
5 The Rich Man and Lazarus (The Afterlife) 65
6 Legion (Valuing People) 81
7 The Centurion (Faith That Amazes God) 97
8 Thomas (The Exclusivity of Jesus for Salvation) 115

Foreword

SOME PEOPLE ARE simply unforgettable. By their mere appearance, mannerisms, or speech they can make an impression that leaves an indelible mark and provides a distinctive memory. My mentor and the founder of Jews for Jesus, Moishe Rosen, was just such a man. At six foot two, 350 pounds, slightly disheveled, and so soft spoken you'd have to strain to hear his words, Moishe always made an impression, for good or for ill. People often wanted to share with me their "the first time I met Moishe" stories, many of which were downright hilarious.

The author of this book is a similarly memorable character. My great friend Lon Solomon has always seemed to carry himself with a certain confident swagger, a confidence often belied by a charming, self-deprecating sense of humor. With piercing blue eyes, a ready smile, and a slight Southern drawl, Lon always has a witty aphorism or a funny joke with which to punctuate his conversation. More than that, Lon is always speaking encouragingly to everyone he meets about the Bible and about Jesus as though he had just been studying the Scriptures or had just been meeting with Jesus in person. And of course, he has been.

In *People Jesus Met*, Lon's love for the Bible and for his Lord and Savior Jesus sparkles with vibrancy and vitality, perhaps because more than anyone I know, Lon's life was utterly transformed when he became one of those people Jesus met. His salvation story is one of the most remarkable I have ever heard, and perhaps that is one reason why you will gain such a blessing through reading these wonderful stories of transformation.

When believers in Jesus share our stories of faith we often speak of the time when we met Jesus. But this book is titled *People Jesus Met*. The distinction is crucial because it speaks to us of the limitless grace of God. Our lives are not so much transformed because we have the good fortune, intelligence, or chance opportunity to meet the Master, but because He in His infinite love and mercy has chosen to meet us.

As the noted Jewish Philosopher Abraham Heschel wrote, God is in search of man, not the other way around. Indeed, God is so passionately in search of man, He "emptied himself, by taking the form of a servant, being born in the likeness of men. And being found in human form, he humbled himself by becoming obedient to the

Foreword

point of death, even death on a cross. Therefore God has highly exalted him and bestowed on him the name that is above every name, so that at the name of Jesus every knee should bow, in heaven and on earth and under the earth, and every tongue confess that Jesus Christ is Lord, to the glory of God the Father" (Philippians 2:7-10, ESV).

All of humanity has in one way or another been blindly and blithely careening on the pathway of our own making toward eternal banishment from God's presence. But then God chose to meet us in the person of Jesus Christ, arresting us from the path of certain self-destruction. If Jesus meets you, He apprehends you, and if you bow your knee, your life is never the same.

These are the riches of the book you now hold in your hand, an invitation to the greatest wisdom and insight available to humanity. And this is the wisdom Lon Solomon unpacks for us in *People Jesus Met*. As you read, be prepared not only to meet the people Jesus met, but also to have Jesus meet you and allow you to gain the riches and life-changing truths that unfold from a true encounter with "Christ, in whom are hidden all the treasures of wisdom and knowledge" (Colossians 2:3, ESV).

—David Brickner
Executive Chairman, Jews for Jesus

1

Mary and Joseph
(God's Timing)

IT'S VERY INTERESTING that the Bible records very little about Jesus' growing up years with His parents.

Actually, once we get past the account of Jesus' birth and the events of His infancy, the Bible records only one other event involving His mom and dad prior to the beginning of Jesus' public ministry at the age of roughly thirty. This is the event we want to talk about in this chapter.

The Bible says, "[Jesus'] parents went to Jerusalem every year at the Feast of the Passover" (Luke 2:41 NKJV). The Old Testament Law required Israelites to make a pilgrimage to Jerusalem for three festivals a year: the Feast of *Tabernacles* (Sukkot), the Feast of *Weeks* (Shavuot), and the Feast of *Passover* (Pesach). The trip from Jesus' hometown of Nazareth was about 100 miles, and people normally traveled in caravans for safety.

The Bible goes on to say, "And when He was twelve years old, they went up to Jerusalem according to the custom of the feast. When they had finished the days, as they returned, the Boy Jesus lingered behind in Jerusalem. And Joseph and His mother did not know it" (Luke 2:42–43 NKJV).

One might wonder how Mary and Joseph could've left Jerusalem and started traveling home without knowing their son was missing. The reason relates to how these traveling caravans worked. The women and children normally traveled at the front of the caravan, and the men brought up the rear for protection. Often the two groups would not see each other all day until they made camp for the night. Since Jesus was twelve years old, He was right on the dividing line between a child and a man (to be bar mitzvahed at age thirteen) in Israelite society. So it is easy to see how each parent might've assumed that Jesus was with the other group.

When Joseph and Mary met up at the end of the day and realized their son was not with them, the Bible says, "So when they did not find Him [in the caravan], they returned to Jerusalem, seeking Him. Now, so it was, that after three days they found Him in the temple, sitting in the midst of the teachers, both listening to them and asking them questions. And all who heard Him were astonished at His understanding and answers" (Luke 2:45–47 NKJV).

Luke 2:48–49 then goes on to say, "So when they [His parents] saw Him, they were amazed; and His mother said to Him, 'Son, why have You done this to us? Look, Your father and I have sought You anxiously.' And He said to them, 'Why did you seek Me? Did you not know that I must be about My Father's business?'" In other words, Jesus said to them, "Don't you understand that I have a special mission from God?"

But they did not understand. Luke 2:50–51 says, "But they did not understand the statement which He spoke to them. Then He went down with them and came to Nazareth, and was subject to them, but His mother kept all these things in her heart."

The next time we hear of Jesus in the Bible is eighteen years later, when God's timing was fully mature for Jesus to carry out His special mission.

This leaves with a question: "**So what**? What does anything in this passage have to do with my life?"

Remember we said earlier that this is the only event from Jesus' childhood with Mary and Joseph that the Bible records. So, out of all the events of Jesus' first thirty years on earth, why would God choose this one particular event to record in the Bible? The answer is because it contains a great spiritual lesson for us as followers of Jesus today.

Even at age twelve, Jesus sensed God's divine call on His life. He sensed the special mission that God had sent Him to earth to carry out. And by sparring with the rabbis at the temple that day, one can sense Jesus' chomping at the bit to launch into this mission.

But God's timing for this mission was not right yet. And it would not be right for another eighteen years! In other words, we could say that Jesus had "the **right job** but the **wrong time**," and God used Jesus' parents to indicate this to Him: "We're asking you to come home to Nazareth, son."

In that moment, Jesus had a choice to make, didn't He? He could forge ahead in *His own timing*, or He could submit to *God's timing* being gently whispered to Him by the Holy Spirit through His parents. Wisely, Jesus chose the latter.

This is the spiritual principle and lesson that God wants us to learn from this encounter between Jesus and His parents. God wants to teach us that **with God, timing is everything**.

Mary and Joseph (God's Timing)

It's taken me a long time to learn this lesson. It's been a challenge for me to learn that identifying the right job or mission is only half of the issue with God. The other half—and very often more important half—is identifying the right timing: **God's timing!** And I'm learning to joyfully submit to God's timing, even though it's almost never mine!

Sooner or later, every seasoned man or woman of God must come to understand this. Moses had to learn this lesson, didn't he?

"When Moses was forty years old, he decided to visit his own people, the Israelites. He saw one of them being mistreated by an Egyptian, so he went to his defense and avenged him by killing the Egyptian. Moses thought that his own people would realize that God was using him to rescue them, but they did not, … After forty years had passed, an angel appeared to Moses in the flames of a burning bush in the desert near Mount Sinai" (Acts 7:23–25, 30 NIV).

"This Moses whom they rejected, saying, 'Who made you a ruler and a judge?' is the one God sent to be a ruler and a deliverer by the hand of the Angel who appeared to him in the bush" (Acts 7:35 NKJV).

As we say: "Moses had *the right job*—he just had *the wrong time*." He knew what God had called him to do; it's just that he was forty years too early!

Let's all be honest and agree: with very few exceptions, when it comes to God's timing, we're all prone to make the same mistake as Moses. We pray and seek God and get a sense of what His will is for some situation, but we're not content to wait on God's timing. We want it done NOW—like yesterday—like ASAP.

More blessings are lost in the Christian life because we're unwilling to wait on God's timing than for any other single reason. The Lord Jesus understood this, which is why at age twelve, when God used parental authority to say to Him, "Hey, Jesus, it's the right job but the wrong time," Jesus submitted to God's timing without dispute.

Nehemiah understood this principle, too. He had heard about the broken-down walls of Jerusalem. He believed that it was God's will for him to go to Jerusalem and rebuild those walls, but instead of running to Persian King Artaxerxes in fleshly impetuosity and asking for permission to go, Nehemiah prayed about this and laid it before God and waited for *months* for God's perfect timing. Finally, the king himself brought it up and fell

Mary and Joseph (God's Timing)

all over himself to give Nehemiah all the assistance he needed to rebuild Jerusalem's wall.

Ruth also understood this principle. Naomi had two sons. Their names in Hebrew were Mahlyon and Chilyon, which means "weakly" and "sickly," and Ruth was married to one of these sons.

"Weakly" and "Sickly" both died. Being a widow in the ancient Near East was a really bad thing. Without a husband or a son to provide for her, a widow was in dire straits. Despite this, instead of running out and grabbing another husband in fleshly impetuousness, Ruth decided to accompany Naomi back to Bethlehem and wait on God's timing for a man.

This is why Ruth was out in the field picking up charity droppings ("gleaning"; see Deuteronomy 24:19-22) when the owner of the field, Boaz, first saw her and proceeded to marry her. Not only did Ruth get a wonderful man who provided for her and Naomi all the days of their lives, but she also became the great-grandmother of a man named David—and so became the great, great, great (etc.) grandmother of the Lord Jesus Himself. All of this happened because Ruth was willing to wait on God's timing and not charge off in her own timing.

Joseph understood this principle, too. God's timing for him involved thirteen years in jail in Egypt, and he patiently waited and became the prime minister of Egypt—in time!

And there was also **David**, for whom God's timing involved seven years of hiding in caves from King Saul—and he patiently waited and eventually became king of Israel in Saul's place.

But there are some folks in the Bible who got this wrong. One example is **Moses** (whom we already mentioned).

Abraham got it wrong, too. He knew God had promised him a son, but instead of waiting on God's timing for this son—even though that timing was twenty-five years later—Abraham "jumped the gun" and took Hagar, Sarah's handmaid, and fathered Ishmael, the father of all Arab people.

When I think of this biblical principle, I'm reminded of Kurt Warner, who led the Arizona Cardinals to win the Super Bowl. Talk about a guy who learned to wait on God's timing! Coming out of high school, he was snubbed by every major university. He was finally taken by the University of Northern Iowa where he played quarterback. As a college senior, he was passed over

Mary and Joseph (God's Timing)

in the NFL draft, so he took a job stocking shelves in a grocery store. It was here that he met his wife Brenda, who led him to Christ in 1995.

For two years, Warner played arena football. Then he played in the European league. Finally, in 1998, the St. Louis Rams signed him as a backup quarterback to Trent Green. Early in the 1999 season, Green was injured. And so, in God's perfect timing, Kurt Warner became the starting quarterback for the Rams and had one of the greatest seasons in NFL history. He led the Rams to win Super Bowl XXXIV and was chosen as MVP of the NFL that year.

As followers of Jesus, all of us, at some point in our lives, have had to struggle with the same conflict between God's timing and our timing that Kurt Warner did.

Maybe you planned to be married by now—but in God's timing, you're still single.

Maybe you planned to have that new job or promotion—but in God's timing, you're still working menial jobs.

Maybe you planned to be financially secure—but in God's timing, you're not.

Maybe you planned to have a house full of children running around by now—but in God's timing, you don't.

Maybe you planned to go to a certain college—but in God's timing, it didn't work out.

Maybe you planned to make it onto a ball team or cheerleading squad—but in God's timing, you were cut.

Maybe you had great plans for your children's future—but in God's timing, they're struggling right now.

And possibly, in His timing, God gave you a child with disabilities who will never come close to the plans you dreamed for that child.

So, as followers of Christ, what do we do with all of this?

Proverbs 16:9 says, "A man's heart plans his way, but the Lord directs his steps" (NKJV).

This is the worldview of a true man or woman of God. Such a person understands Isaiah 55:8: "'For My thoughts are not your thoughts, nor are your ways My ways,' says the Lord" (NJKV). Neither is God's timing our timing.

True men and women of God understand that God has better ways of getting them to where they need to be, when they need to be there, than they could ever plan for themselves. These men and women live by faith, which means that they trust and obey God even when they don't understand exactly what He's doing or why. And

Mary and Joseph (God's Timing)

just as importantly, they submit to the timing of God in their lives, whether they understand it or not. They do this because they are totally confident that not only is **God's will** for their lives perfect, but **God's timing** for their lives is also perfect.

And, as followers of Jesus, this is precisely how God is calling us to live.

Now, one might ask, "Okay, Lon, I understand the point, but have one final question: How do I know when God is telling me to **act** and when He is telling me to **wait**? How do I know when God's timing is now and when it isn't?

That's an excellent question. I cannot give you an exact formula, but I can give you three guidelines.

Guideline #1—Circumstances. God often uses our circumstances to make it clear that we are to wait, like Joseph being stuck in jail or David being forced to hide in caves or Moses being in exile in the Sinai desert, or when we don't get that raise or don't get into that college or aren't able to get pregnant.

When God does this, it's critical that we recognize that God's trying to tell us that His timing is not yet ripe, that we submit to His timing, and that we resist the temptation to take matters into our own hands.

Guideline #2—Authority. Sometimes God uses people in authority over us to make it clear that God's timing is not yet right, such as the boss who passes us over for that promotion or the parents who say "no" to us or the church leaders who refuse to give us that leadership role.

This is exactly how the Lord communicated to young Jesus that the timing of God was not yet right. And just as Jesus cheerfully submitted to God through the authority of His parents, so too must we submit to those in authority.

Guideline #3—Time with God. We often get the signal that we must wait on God's timing by being on our knees, deeply and intimately seeking the Lord. This kind of signal from God may come in a "still, small voice," but once we have heard it, it allows us to say in a bold, loud voice, "I know that God's will for me right now is just to wait on His perfect timing." This is why I urge you to have a serious quiet time with the Lord, so you can cultivate this intimacy with Him and you can hear His "still, small voice" for yourself.

What have we learned today? **With God, timing is everything.**

Mary and Joseph (God's Timing)

Therefore, as Christ followers, we not only must ask, "Have I discerned God's **will** for this situation?" but also, "Have I discerned God's **timing** for this situation?"

In closing, one last suggestion: "If in doubt, wait!" Very seldom have I ever regretted waiting a little longer to act until I was sure of God's timing, but I sure have regretted moving ahead too soon.

I'll leave you with King David's words of wisdom from Psalm 27:14: "Wait for the Lord; be strong and let your heart take courage; yes, wait for the Lord" (NASB).

2

Satan (Scripture Memory)

LET'S SAY YOU'RE an investment banker and you've just closed a huge deal, so you head out to have a celebratory lunch on the bank. How big of a temptation would it be for you to be just a little too extravagant on the bank's dime?

Well, a few years ago, for five London bankers from Barclays, I'm afraid the temptation was too great. After closing a big deal, they went to a top London restaurant and ordered some of the most expensive wine in the world, and then they kept on ordering it again and again until, by the time they were done, their bill for the wine was so high that the restaurant owner gave them their food for free!

How much was their lunchtime wine bill? Would you believe $65,000? Needless to say, the officials at Barclays Bank didn't see a lot of humor in this situation. In fact, they fired all five bankers!

Temptation. It means to be enticed to do something that you know you shouldn't—something you know you're going to be sorry for in the morning. For me, my toughest temptation every day is overeating. I grew up in a highly dysfunctional home where I learned to "eat my pain away." So often, I end my day feeling like the lady I saw on a Weight Watchers commercial. She said, "I have lots of willpower when it comes to food. It's just that right now, I'm not using any of it."

Whether it's food or alcohol or pornography or drugs or sex or lust or gossip or spending too much money shopping—all of us are in mortal combat with our own personal set of temptations every day. If we're honest, most of us would have to admit that we lose these battles a lot more than we win them.

This is what we want to talk about in this chapter: temptation and the weapons God has given us as followers of Jesus so that we can win these battles more often than we lose them.

"Then [after Jesus was baptized by John the Baptist] Jesus was led up by the Spirit into the wilderness to be tempted by the devil" (Matthew 4:1 NKJV).

Those of you who have been to Israel have probably seen the area around Jericho between Jerusalem and the Dead Sea. It's an arid, parched, ragged desert—and

Satan (Scripture Memory)

the Bible says that the Holy Spirit led Jesus out into this desert to be tempted by the devil himself.

We should stop for a moment and ask: "Why was the devil trying to tempt Jesus into sinning?"

The reason was this: If Satan could get Jesus to commit even one sin, he could extinguish God's plan of salvation forever.

God's plan of salvation is based on the principle of "substitutionary atonement." This means that God is willing to let a substitute atone for your sin and my sin and everyone else's sin with one condition: this substitute has to be without blemish—perfect and sinless and holy. God's holy justice cannot let someone pay our "death penalty for sin" if that person owes the very same death penalty; and the only way to owe **no** death penalty for sin is for a person to have never sinned in the first place.

So, if Jesus was to be our "atoning substitute" who bore and paid for our sins on the cross, then it was absolutely imperative that He be perfectly sinless Himself. As the Bible says, "For you know that it was not with perishable things such as silver or gold that you were redeemed from the empty way of life handed down to you from your ancestors, but with the precious blood of Christ, a lamb without blemish or defect" (1 Peter 1:18–19 NIV).

Even one sin on Jesus' part would cause God's entire plan of salvation to go up in smoke—and Satan knew it!

"After fasting forty days and forty nights, he was hungry. The tempter came to him and said, 'If you are the Son of God, tell these stones to become bread'" (Matthew 4:2–3 NIV).

First, the devil challenged Jesus to do a miracle to relieve His craving for food. Now, there is nothing wrong with making bread for ourselves, but there was much more than that going on here. Jesus had been led by the Holy Spirit (Matthew 4:1) into the wilderness and directed to fast. In other words, it was God's will that Jesus go without food at this moment. Therefore, what the devil was really asking Jesus to do was to take matters into His own hands—to assert His own independent will above God's will for His life.

We must understand that this is one of the most common ways that the enemy tempts us. We all have the natural desire for sex, intimacy, money, material things, notoriety, and success. There is nothing wrong with these desires so long as we satisfy them within the will of God for our lives; but what Satan was tempting Jesus to do—and what Satan tempts you to do—is to satisfy these normal human desires outside of God's will for our lives, which is disobedient to God and sinful in the Lord's holy sight, as well as self-destructive and counter-productive in our lives.

Jesus answered, "It is written [Deuteronomy 8:3], 'Man shall not live by bread alone, but by every word that proceeds from the mouth of God'" (Matthew 4:4 NKJV).

Look how Jesus counteracted Satan's attack: **"It is written."** Jesus quoted Scripture to the devil in response to his attempt to lure Jesus into sin. Essentially, Jesus said, "Hey, Satan, it's better to be hungry **in** the will of God than to be satisfied **outside** the will of God." After forty days without food, this had to be a huge temptation that Jesus resisted here. Where did He get the power to do this? He got it by quoting Scripture.

"Then the devil took Him up into the holy city [Jerusalem], set Him on the pinnacle of the temple, and said to Him, 'If You are the Son of God, throw Yourself down. For it is written [Psalm 91:11]: "He shall give His angels charge over you," and, "In their hands they shall bear you up, lest you dash your foot against a stone"'" (Matthew 4:5–6 NKJV).

In this second temptation, Satan appealed to Jesus' **pride.** He took Him to the temple in Jerusalem and had Him stand on the pinnacle of the temple mount—this is the southeast corner where the drop into the Kidron Valley below is a hundred feet.

Here Satan said to Jesus, "Hey, Jesus, if You were to jump and miraculously float to a safe landing in the valley below, all the Jewish people would hail You as the Messiah for sure! You'd be the biggest story in town. You'd be on the front page of every newspaper. Hey, You're the Son of God—You deserve this kind of attention and recognition."

"Jesus said to him, 'It is written again [Deuteronomy 6:16], "You shall not tempt the Lord your God"'" (Matthew 4:7 NKJV).

Once again, Satan attacked Jesus in an area where he knew that we're all vulnerable as human beings: our pride and ego and desire for attention and notoriety.

Living here in the Washington, DC, area, I see this human weakness on display every day. Over the almost fifty years that I have lived here, I have seen Satan and his demons destroy one life after another in this place by using the almost irresistible aphrodisiacs of power, influence, and "big-shot status," but once again, Jesus resisted Satan's temptation by using the same weapon: **"It is written!"** Jesus said to him, "Yes, God does promise to protect me—but not when I plunge myself into a sensationalistic, foolish situation aimed only at inflating my own ego and sinful human pride."

"Again, the devil took Him up on an exceedingly high mountain, and showed Him all the kingdoms of the world and their glory. And he said to Him, 'All these things I will give You if You will fall down and worship me'" (Matthew 4:8–9 NKJV).

In this third temptation, Satan appealed to Jesus' human desire to avoid pain, hardship, and suffering. God had already promised to give Jesus the throne of all the kingdoms of the world: "He [God the Father] said to me [Jesus], 'You are my son; today I have become your father. Ask me, and I will make the nations your inheritance, the ends of the earth your possession'" (Psalm 2:7–8 NIV). However, Jesus was on His way to this throne by way of the cross!

Death by crucifixion was one of the most gruesome ways to die that man has ever concocted. The Romans did not invent it, but they perfected it. Essentially, a man's strength ebbed away until he could no longer expand his diaphragm muscle and breathe. His circulation became poor, and he basically drowned in his own bodily fluids.

The cross meant more than this for Jesus. On the cross, for the first time in history, He, the second person in the Godhead, was to be separated from the Father for a moment while the sins of the world were laid upon Him. The spiritual pain in this separation would be even greater than the physical pain.

The Bible records for us the events in the Garden of Gethsemane, where we are told that the anticipation of both the physical and spiritual pain of the cross was a real issue for Jesus. He prayed, "Father, if it is Your will, take this cup away from Me" (Luke 22:42 NKJV).

So, here in the third temptation, Satan showed up with an enticing counterproposal for Jesus becoming the ruler of all the world—one that skipped the cross and all its pain. It was an offer that, by the way, skipped God's plan of salvation for the human race, too!

Certainly, this offer presented the Lord Jesus with a real temptation. As human beings, we all want to detour around the hard times of life and take the easy way. But when we want to do this so badly that we rebel against and reject God's divine plan for our lives, that's a problem, because that's sin! This is precisely what the devil was tempting Jesus to do.

"Then Jesus said to him, 'Away with you, Satan! For **it is written** [Deuteronomy 6:13], "You shall worship

Satan (Scripture Memory)

the Lord your God, and Him only you shall serve'"'" (Matthew 4:10 NKJV).

In other words, Jesus said to him, "I'm going to worship God and embrace His plan for My life. If that plan calls for Me to hang on a cross before I can sit on the throne, then so be it! I'm not interested in your sinful shortcuts."

"Then the devil left Him, and behold, angels came and ministered to Him" (Matthew 4:11 NKJV).

What a wonderful passage of Scripture, assuring us that our Savior is indeed the sinless Son of God who was qualified to take our sins away by His work on the cross for us!

All of this leads us to ask: "**So what?** Lon, what does all this have to do with my everyday life as a follower of Jesus?"

In the Bible, James 4:7 says, "Resist the devil, and he will flee from you" (NIV). This is a promise from God that we can claim in protecting ourselves against the devil and fighting off his temptations.

So, let's ask the question: "How did Jesus 'resist the devil' here in Matthew chapter 4?"

The answer is this: When faced with temptation, Jesus recalled a verse of Scripture that applied to that specific temptation and quoted it to Himself and to the devil: "It is written ... it is written ... it is written."

The point is that, as followers of Jesus Christ, in our fight against temptation, so often we try to use the wrong weapons. We try to use our human willpower, grit, and determination. We try to "gut it out." We walk out of the house every day and say in the energy of our human willpower, "I will not lust, I will not eat too much, I will not gossip, I will not judge others so harshly..." and we fail miserably.

The reason we fail is because these are not the weapons that God has created and given us to fight temptation. To put it simply: The energy of the flesh cannot defeat the power of the flesh, nor can it defeat the temptations of the devil.

But the great news of the Bible is that, as followers of Jesus, God has given us weapons—spiritual weapons—that will work against both the power of the flesh and the temptations of the devil. Here in Matthew chapter 4, the Lord Jesus illustrates this spiritual weaponry to us and shows us exactly how to use it.

Regarding this passage, the great Church Father Origen said, "Jesus routed the tempter with a weapon that we can all use, the sword of the Spirit, which is the

Satan (Scripture Memory)

Word of God. We must learn from this passage the power of scripture and the impotence of Satan against it."

Indeed, the entire Bible testifies to this truth:

- Ephesians 6:11 NIV: "Put on the full armor of God, so that you can take your stand against the devil's schemes." The only offensive weapon in the armor that the Bible lists (Ephesians 6:14–17) is the sword of the Spirit, which is the Word of God (i.e., Scripture).
- Hebrews 4:12 NKJV: "For the word of God is living and powerful, and sharper than any two-edged sword."
- 2 Corinthians 10:3–4 ESV: "For though we walk in the flesh, we are not waging war according to the flesh. For the weapons of our warfare are not of the flesh but have divine power to destroy strongholds."

The bottom line as followers of Jesus is that when we resist temptation in our lives as the Lord Jesus did in His life—not with human grit or guts or determination, but with, "It is written … it is written … it is written…"—that's when we'll have the same results that He did!

We do this in our everyday lives exactly the way that Jesus did. We figure out the areas in life where we face our greatest temptations to sin, and then we find verses in the Bible that speak to those specific areas. Then we memorize those verses, and then, when facing a temptation, we pull those verses out and quote them out loud to the devil and to the temptation and to ourselves.

Do this and you will be amazed at the power that wells up within you to fight off your worst temptations, because now you're fighting with God's spiritual weaponry that He has endowed (2 Corinthians 2:10) with divine power—namely, the living, powerful, external Word of God.

For example, **LUST**: memorize 1 Thessalonians 4:3–4, 7: "It is God's will that you should be sanctified: that you should avoid sexual immorality; that each of you should learn to control your own body in a way that is holy and honorable. ... For God did not call us to be impure, but to live a holy life" (NIV).

Then there's **FEAR**: memorize Isaiah 43:1–4: "Do not fear. ... When you pass through the waters, I will be with you; and when you pass through the rivers, they will not sweep over you. When you walk through the fire, you will not be burned; the flames will not set you ablaze.

Satan (Scripture Memory)

For I am the Lord your God. ... You are precious and honored in my sight" (NIV). God gave my wife Brenda this passage of Scripture while she was carrying our fourth child, Jill. Our daughter's birth has been followed by thirty-two years of severe disabilities, thousands of seizures, hospitalizations, sleepless nights, and fears of every kind—yet Brenda and I have quoted this passage at our fears for the last thirty-two years, and by the grace of God, we're still standing, and my daughter is doing better than she ever has.

Then there's **GOSSIP**: memorize Ephesians 4:29: "Do not let any unwholesome talk come out of your mouths, but only what is helpful for building others up according to their needs, that it may benefit those who listen" (NIV). Quote this five times before you open your mouth to speak about another person, and I'll bet no nastiness comes out.

Then there's **LEWD SPEECH**: memorize Ephesians 5:3–4: "But among you there must not be even a hint of sexual immorality, or of any kind of impurity, or of greed, because these are improper for God's holy people. Nor should there be obscenity, foolish talk or coarse joking, which are out of place, but rather thanksgiving" (NIV). Repeat this passage to yourself when things turn dirty at the water cooler, and I'll bet you'll find the courage to walk away and not join in, no matter what the others may think of you.

Then there's **LAZINESS**: memorize Colossians 3:23–24: "Whatever you do, work at it with all your heart, as working for the Lord, not for human masters. ... It is the Lord Christ you are serving" (NIV). When you're tempted to cut corners at work or at anything, throw this verse at it.

Then there's **SCHEMING**: memorize Luke 12:2–3: "There is nothing concealed that will not be disclosed, or hidden that will not be made known. What you have said in the dark will be heard in the daylight, and what you have whispered in the ear in the inner rooms will be proclaimed from the roofs" (NIV). This will make you think twice before plotting evil.

We could go on, but I believe the point is clear. For every temptation, there's an "it is written" in the Bible. Our task is to do what Jesus did: find it, memorize it, and then use it against the tempter and his evil friends.

In fact, I should point out that in Matthew chapter 4, two of the verses of Scripture that Jesus quoted to the devil come from Deuteronomy chapter 6, and the other is from Deuteronomy chapter 8. This tells us that even as the Lord was spending forty days alone in the wilderness, He was clearly meditating on and memorizing the book of Deuteronomy, maybe even reading a copy He had taken with Him. He was doing this so that, when Satan's attack came upon Him, He was spiritually fortified and prepared to ward it off. If the living Messiah needed to do this, how much more do we?

You might say, "Lon, all this sounds way too simple." Well, it *is* simple—but God promises it'll work! So why keep holding on to your complicated plan for fighting temptation and failing when you can use God's simple plan and succeed?

Be careful not to be educated beyond your intelligence!

Conclusion

Let's conclude by saying that this is why any good pastor and church will be constantly urging you to be reading the Scriptures and studying them and meditating on them.

Even more, they'll be urging you to be memorizing Scripture, because, when we're being tempted to sin, we can't throw Scripture at the devil and the temptation that we don't know!

This is why King David said, "Your word I have hidden in my heart [memorized], that I might not sin against You" (Psalm 119:11 NKJV).

When I was a brand-new believer in Jesus in the spring of 1971, my life exhibited a most dramatic turnaround. Many people asked me how I explained such a radical change. I told them that I had begun memorizing verses of Scripture since I was first saved and that I had committed to memory over 600 verses of Scripture by the time I was six months old in the Lord. I would carry them on index cards in my pocket and review them all the time. I used every spare moment I had to pull them out and review them. In other words, I hid lots of God's Word in my heart (Psalm 119:11), and that produced lots of God-honoring change in my life.

Allow me to issue you a challenge: make it your goal to memorize one verse of scripture (the words and the location in the Bible) per week. Review them all once a week, and the same thing that happened to me will happen to you!

3

The Paralytic (Mark 2:1–12) (Jesus' Authority to Forgive Sin)

IF I WERE to ask you, "What was the most distinctive message that Dr. Martin Luther King, Jr., proclaimed?" I think most of us would get it right: **"Equality for all people."**

If I were to ask you what Mother Theresa's most distinctive message was, I believe most people would know the answer: **"The poor children of the world matter to God."**

Gandhi's most distinctive message was: **"Nonviolence is the best way to bring about political change."**

But what if I were to ask you, "What was the most distinctive message that the Lord Jesus Christ proclaimed when He was here on earth?"

The answer: **"I have the authority to forgive your sin."**

In fact, this is the most distinctive message that biblical Christianity proclaims to the people of the world. It's true that Christianity offers us a noble way to live. It's also true that it offers us some great examples to model our lives after, including Paul and Peter and Mary and Martha.

The central message of the Bible has nothing to do with noble ethics or great behavioral models. Rather, it's that Almighty God is offering to forgive the sin of every human being and grant them eternal life and heaven. But this offer is available only through faith in Jesus Christ.

This is what we want to talk about in Chapter 3.

Let's begin by asking the basic question: "What exactly is sin, anyway?"

For the answer to this question, we need to go all the way back to the first sin ever committed in the universe. Sin did not begin with Adam or Eve in the Garden of Eden. It began with an angel we know today as Lucifer, also called "Satan" in the Bible (which in Hebrew means "adversary").

The Bible says in Isaiah 14:12, "How you are fallen from heaven, O Lucifer, son of the morning!" (NKJV). According to the Bible, Lucifer was originally a prominent angel. Ezekiel 28:15 says, "You were blameless in your ways ... till wickedness was found in you" (NIV). And what kind of wickedness was it? Isaiah 14:13–14

(Jesus' Authority to Forgive Sin)

says, "You said in your heart, 'I will ascend to the heavens; I will raise my throne above the stars of God; I will sit enthroned on the mount of assembly. ... I will make myself like the Most High" (NIV).

Did you notice the keyword here? It's "I." **My** way, **my** will, **my** glory, **ME, ME, ME!**

The essence of Satan's sin was his decision that God was not going to be the Lord of his life but that he was going to be his own lord. This, in a nutshell, is what sin is all about. And not just one angel did this. The Bible tells us in Revelation 12:7–9 that there were a number of angels who allied themselves with him.

What was God's response? Look at Isaiah 14:15: "Yet you [Lucifer] shall be brought down to Sheol, to the lowest depths of the Pit" (NKJV). God was not about to tolerate such rebellion. So God created a place of everlasting torment for Lucifer and his demonic, evil angels—and also for any other beings in the universe who might choose to follow Satan in what John Milton referred to as "his foul revolt."

We might wonder what all this has to do with us human beings. Well, much in every way! Sin did not stop with Lucifer. Instead, he lured Adam and Eve into copying his rebellion against God.

God had commanded Adam and Eve not to eat of the Tree of the Knowledge of Good and Evil, located in the Garden of Eden, lest they surely die; but along came Lucifer and he said to them, "You will not surely die. For God knows that in the day you eat of it your eyes will be opened, and will be like God, knowing good and evil" (Genesis 3:4–5 NKJV).

Notice Lucifer's appeal to Adam and Eve:

- They could **become their own gods.**
- They could **decide their own destiny.**
- They could **run their own lives their own way.**

Adam and Eve "took the bait." They sinned.

It gets worse. The Bible tells us in Romans 5:12, "Wherefore, as by one man sin entered into the world, and death by sin; and so death passed upon all men, for that all have sinned" (KJV). The Bible says that because of Adam and Eve's sin, the entire human race became infected with an inbred "sin nature," so that every member of Adam and Eve's race is born a "sinner" in the sight of the all-holy God of this universe.

The Bible says that the result of Adam and Eve's sin was condemnation for all men, for by the disobedience

(Jesus' Authority to Forgive Sin)

of one man (Adam), we were all made sinners (Romans 5:18–19). This is why King David said, "Surely I was sinful at birth, sinful from the time my mother conceived me" (Psalm 51:5 NIV).

As a result, every one of us enters this world as a rebel against God, determined to go our own way, determined to be our own masters—just like Lucifer. This is why the Bible says, "All of us, like sheep, have gone astray, each of us has turned to his own way" (Isaiah 53:6 NASB).

If you don't believe that this is the true nature of the human spirit, just spend a couple of days in the same house with a two-year-old and you'll see! *"No, no, no!" "Mine, mine, mine!"* Here we see the real spirit of mankind in all its fury, and it doesn't change just because we become adults.

Whether we're two or eighty-two, so long as we decide that we are going to reign supreme over our lives and not God, He will regard us as "sinners" and as followers of Lucifer in his "foul revolt." That's a big problem! Because remember what we've already learned—that not only is God going to send Lucifer to hell for all eternity—but also all those who follow him in his rebellion against God.

So this is the disease—and we've all got it!

But the Bible has some really "Good News" for us! The "Good News" is that God has made a way for our sin to be forgiven. He has made a way for us sinners to be pardoned and acquitted.

Who has the authority to do this for us? We're about to find out in Mark chapter 2.

"A few days later, when Jesus again entered Capernaum, the people heard that he had come home. They gathered in such large numbers that there was no room left, not even outside the door" (Mark 2:1–2 NIV). Growing up, I remember that my dad had a favorite phrase he loved to use, that people were "packed in like sardines." This is precisely what the Bible is telling us here in Mark: that the crowd in Capernaum filled the house where Jesus was and then spilled out of the house and onto the street.

This information is critical for us to know because it explains what happens next.

"Then they came to Him, bringing a paralytic who was carried by four men. And … they could not come near Him because of the crowd" (Mark 2:3 NKJV). It takes a fairly large aisle for four men and a stretcher to get through. To make matters worse, people weren't very much in the mood for moving over and letting them by.

(Jesus' Authority to Forgive Sin)

So instead, these four friends of the paralyzed man came up with a rather ingenious way to get around the problem.

"They uncovered the roof where He was. So when they had broken through, they let down the bed on which the paralytic was lying" (Mark 2:4 NKJV). In those days, roofs of houses around the Sea of Galilee were flat so people could sit and enjoy the cool breeze off the sea. These houses had stairs on the outside going up to the roof. And so, huffing and puffing and sweating and straining, these four men hoisted their paralyzed friend up onto the roof, and when they finally got there, they began to chop a hole in it. This wasn't a little hole, either—it was big enough to lower a full-grown man through while he was lying flat on a stretcher! When it was all over, this paralyzed man was lying flat on his back at the feet of Jesus.

"When Jesus saw their faith, he said to the paralyzed man, 'Son, your sins are forgiven'" (Mark 2:5 NIV).

The word Jesus used here in the Greek New Testament is **aphiemi**. This means to dismiss, remove, or cancel something.

The tense of this verb that Jesus used in Mark 2:5 is critically important. He used the perfect tense in Greek. This tense is not used abundantly in the Greek New

Testament, which means that when it is used, it is meant to be emphatic.

In koine Greek (the Greek of the New Testament), the perfect tense is used for a past completed action, the results of which go on for eternity. One could describe the perfect tense as a dot (past completed action) with a line coming out and stretching to infinity (eternal results of the action). Therefore, what Jesus really said to this paralyzed man was, "Son, your sins have been canceled, are now canceled, and will remain canceled **for all eternity**!" In other words, the blackboard with your sins written on it has been erased forever. So what Jesus was talking about here was an absolute, total, permanent dismissal of this man's sin in God's judicial sight—forever!

I have been told that when the first missionaries went to the Eskimos, they encountered a problem: there was no word in the Eskimo language for "forgiveness." Eventually, the missionaries learned a one-word Eskimo phrase that goes like this: "**I-su-ma-gi-ju-jung- na-e-ner-muk**." This phrase means, "Not being able to think about it anymore," and this is what they used to translate the word "forgiveness" throughout the Bible, because this is exactly how the Bible says God forgives our sins.

(Jesus' Authority to Forgive Sin)

- "As far as the east is from the west, so far has He removed our transgressions from us" (Psalm 103:12 NKJV).
- "You will cast all our sins into the depths of the sea" (Micah 7:19 NKJV).
- "Their sin I will remember no more" (Jeremiah 31:34 NKJV).

This is what the Lord Jesus gave this paralyzed man in Mark chapter 2. And this is what Jesus offers to do for you and me and every person alive: to **"I-su-ma-gi-ju-jung- na-e-ner-muk"** our sin. The Bible is emphatic on this point: that God offers to do this only for people who have placed their total trust for the forgiveness of their sins in Jesus and what He did on the cross for them—shedding His blood to pay for our sins in the sight of a Holy God. As the Apostle said, "Through Jesus the forgiveness of sins is proclaimed to you. Through Him everyone who believes is set free from every sin" (Acts 13:38–39 NIV).

"And some of the scribes [Jewish teachers of the law] were sitting there and thinking in their hearts, 'Why does this Man speak blasphemies like this? Who can forgive sins but God alone?'" (Mark 2:6 NKJV).

Now, for once, the Jewish religious leaders got something right, didn't they? Indeed, God—and God alone—can forgive sin. But the problem was that these guys didn't recognize the incarnate God of the universe when He was standing right in front of them in the Person of Jesus!

And in their objection to Jesus' promise to forgive this paralyzed man, they were issuing a challenge to Jesus to prove that He could really do this.

"But immediately, when Jesus perceived in His spirit that they reasoned thus within themselves, He said to them, 'Why do you reason about these things in your hearts? Which is easier, to say to the paralytic, "Your sins are forgiven you," or to say, "Arise, take up your bed and walk"?'" (Mark 2:8–9 NKJV).

Now let's think for a moment. What is the answer to Jesus' question? Well, it's much easier to say to the paralyzed man, "Your sins are forgiven," because how can anyone validate whether what you say to him is true or not?

However, if I walk up to a paralyzed man and say, "Pick up your stretcher and walk," everyone would know within ten seconds whether I can really do this. Either

(Jesus' Authority to Forgive Sin)

the man picks up his stretcher and walks, or he just lies there and stares at me!

Jesus' point is that it's much easier to say to the man lying at his feet, "Your sins are forgiven," because nobody can prove if He is right or wrong.

"'But that you may know that the Son of Man has power on earth to forgive sins,'—He said to the paralytic, 'I say to you, arise, take up your bed, and go to your house'" (Mark 2:10–11 NKJV). In other words, Jesus said to them, "I'm going to prove to you that I can do the easier thing (i.e., forgiving the man's sins) by doing the harder thing (i.e., healing him)."

What a dramatic moment this must have been. Jesus was "putting it all on the line" here. Either he could do **both** things—heal this man *and* forgive his sins—or He could do **neither**!

"He [the paralyzed man] got up [no atrophy, no muscle weakness, but total and complete healing], took his mat and walked out in full view of them all" (Mark 2:12a NIV). Wow, can you just imagine the scene? And I'll bet you he had no trouble getting an aisle to walk out of that place!

"This amazed everyone and they praised God, saying, 'We have never seen anything like this!" (Mark 2:12b NIV).

In summary, the main point here in Mark 2 is not that Jesus healed this paralyzed man—it is what Jesus proved by healing him. He proved that He has the authority to forgive people's sins—to cancel our sins for good—and to remove them from God's memory forever.

This is the "Good News" of the Bible!

All of this causes us to ask: "**So what**? How does any of this affect my everyday life in the twenty-first century?"

A few years ago, in London, the Atheist Bus Campaign began—supported by scientist Richard Dawkins and the British Humanist Society. They placed ads on over 800 buses across Britain that read: "There's probably no God. Now stop worrying and enjoy your life."

Let's think for a moment what this ad is really saying. It's saying that absolute truth (absolute right/wrong) does not exist because there's no divine being to define things as such; therefore, there's no such thing as "sin," and that "eternal accountability for sin" is an empty threat, and that hell is just a myth that the writers of the Bible made up to scare and manipulate people. All of this means that we can stop worrying and live however we want, with no

(Jesus' Authority to Forgive Sin)

fear of having to stand accountable as "sinners" before a holy God—because there *is* no such God!

The only problem with this ad is that its entire operating premise—that there is no God—is incorrect.

Psalm 19:1 tells us, "The heavens declare the glory of God; the skies proclaim the work of his hands" (NIV). The Bible says that all we have to do is look at the sky and the stars and the planets and the galaxies. Anyone with any sense should be able to figure out that there must be a mighty Creator God out there somewhere who made and sustains all of this. As Psalm 14:1 declares, "The fool says in his heart, 'There is no God'" (NIV).

Furthermore, the Bible says, speaking of the human body, "I am fearfully and wonderfully made" (Psalm 139:14 NIV).

I remember speaking with an unbelieving doctor friend of mine and saying, "I don't see how any doctor can be an atheist."

"How so?" he replied.

I said, "Because once you see all the incredibly complex systems that make up the human body, there's no way you can believe that all this 'just happened.'"

He thought for a moment and said, "I ever really thought about it that way."

I replied, "Well, in all due respect, you need to!"

The endocrine system, digestive system, neurological system, reproductive system, cardiovascular system—with all their perfection and precision—can anyone really believe that there isn't a mighty Creator God who made all of this?

If there *is* such a God, then "right and wrong" are real. And sin is real. And every one of us is a "sinner" in the sight of this holy God.

If there *is* such a God, then "eternal accountability for sin" will be enforced, because God says it will. And "hell" is a real place where sinners really go. Therefore, as sinners—contrary to these bus ads—we have every reason to worry!

Now you might say, "Wow, Lon—thanks! Now I'm really depressed." But there's no reason to be depressed, because there's another way for us to "stop worrying and enjoy life" than the way this bus ad suggests. That way is not by denying God and *minimizing* our sin—it's by embracing God and being *forgiven* for our sin.

Jesus said, "If the Son [Jesus Himself] sets you free [from sin], you will be free indeed" (John 8:36 NIV). This is what Jesus did for the paralyzed man—Jesus forgave his sins and set him free from them forever. This is

(Jesus' Authority to Forgive Sin)

precisely what the Bible says Jesus offers to you and me and every person alive.

When Jesus exercises His authority and forgives our sin, let's remember what the Bible says God does:

- He remembers our sins no more (Hebrews 10:17)
- He removes our sins from us as far as the east is from the west (Psalm 103:12)
- He casts our sins into the depths of the sea (Micah 7:19)
- He writes our names in the Lamb's Book of Life forever (Malachi 3:16–18)
- He grants us an absolute, total, permanent pardon for sin (Romans 8:1)
- He sets us free from the guilt of sin, the bondage of sin, the eternal consequences of sin, and the fear of death (Hebrews 2:14–15)

So now we can stop worrying and can enjoy our lives!

Recently, I was laughing with some friends at dinner and then, as the food arrived, they asked me to pray for the food. So I said, "Lord, thank You that as followers of Jesus, we can laugh and enjoy life and live without fear, because we know that our sins are forgiven and are canceled for all eternity by the direct authority of our Risen Lord."

This is the "**So what?**" for this passage: "The Son of Man has the authority on earth to forgive sins" (Mark 2:10 NIV).

Jesus exercises this authority for every person who embraces Him as Lord and Savior. Once He does this for us, we have a legitimate reason to "stop worrying about eternity and start enjoying life." If you're a follower of Jesus today, I want to challenge you to begin reveling and rejoicing every day in the amazing forgiveness of God that's been granted you in the Lord Jesus Christ.

"Then the seventy returned with joy, saying, 'Lord, even the demons are subject to us in Your name.' And He said to them, ,.. 'Do not rejoice in this, that the spirits are subject to you, but rather rejoice because your names are written in heaven'" (Luke 10:17–18, 20).

Right now, I know things are tough for a lot of us—maybe your finances are really tight, or you've lost your job, or you've had to leave your house, or your 401k is decimated, or your marriage is struggling, or your loved one is chronically ill. We all know that the Lord has promised to help us through these challenges and that

(Jesus' Authority to Forgive Sin)

He'll be faithful to His promises, but still, these are real problems with real stress that can really get us down.

Jesus' message to His disciples in Luke chapter 10 is exactly His message to you today: no matter what else is going wrong with your day, so long as your name is "recorded in heaven" because of the awesome eternal forgiveness He granted you by His personal authority, there's *always* something to rejoice about!

4

Matthew
(Following Jesus Correctly)

IN 1966, WHEN I was a freshman at UNC Chapel Hill, I joined one of the thirty-three social fraternities then on campus. It was a group of 90 to 100 male students, 50 percent Jewish and 50 percent Gentile. We were everything that the movie *Animal House* portrayed—and worse!

Then as a junior at Chapel Hill, I got heavily into the drug culture. This included, among other things, smoking marijuana and hashish, taking LSD and a variety of other psychedelic drugs, as well as selling drugs to others on campus. I did this not just for the fun of it, but also because I was searching for some solid answers to life and I thought that the drug culture would enlighten me and lead me to these answers. It didn't.

But then, in the spring of 1971, I gave my life to Jesus Christ. Suddenly, I found all the answers I was looking for: who I was, why I was here, and what was the meaning of my life. I also found the supernatural joy, peace, and wholeness in life that only God Himself can supply.

Almost immediately, I stopped using drugs, cussing, partying, womanizing, and so forth. And I made it my goal to share Jesus with all ninety-something of my fraternity brothers before I left Chapel Hill. Most of them were utterly disinterested. Most of them thought I had totally lost my mind. And I soon became the running joke of the frat house.

Someone might ask, "If your actions made you into an object of such mockery and ridicule, then why did you keep doing it?"

The answer is because Jesus Christ had called me to a whole new life and way of living. And I was determined to follow Him—as fully as I could—regardless of the cost or what people thought of me.

In this chapter, Jesus met a man named Matthew and called him to this same new way of living that He called me to. We want to look at Matthew's response and then talk about what difference it makes to you and me today as followers of Jesus.

The Bible says, "After these things [i.e., the healing of the paralyzed man in our previous chapter] He went out and saw a tax collector named Levi, sitting at the tax office" (Luke 5:27a NKJV).

The Bible tells us that Levi's nickname was Matthew and that he was a tax collector (or as translated in the KJV, a publican).

If I were to ask you, in today's world, to name the most despicable occupation you can think of, I wonder what you might say. Some people might say the owner of a porn shop, or a pimp, or a heroin dealer.

If you could have asked this question of the Jews in Jesus' day, surely 99 out of 100 of them would have given you the exact same answer: "A tax collector." This was a Jewish man who collected taxes for the Roman government, which occupied Israel at that time.

This was the arrangement: as long as the tax collectors handed over the required amount of tax money to the Roman authorities, anything over that amount that they had extracted from their Jewish brethren they could keep for themselves. In other words, these tax collectors were licensed to engage in legalized extortion. And because they were backed up by the Roman army, Jewish people had no choice but to pay whatever they demanded. As a result, most of the tax collectors became filthy rich.

So you can see why the Jewish people in Israel hated tax collectors with a passion. They considered them traitors against their own people. They were not allowed to enter a synagogue, their testimony was inadmissible in court, and the rabbis forbade Jewish people from even talking to them on the street.

You might ask further, "Who did these tax collectors hang out with?" They kept company with other tax collectors and with prostitutes and drunks and criminals—that is, with all the other outcasts in Jewish society. This is critical for us to know, because it explains what happened a little later on in Luke chapter 5.

The Bible continues: "And He [Jesus] said to him [Matthew], 'Follow me.' So he left all, rose up, and followed Him" (Luke 5:27b-28 NKJV). And the Bible is clear that Matthew never came back.

The story isn't over yet! "Then Levi held a great banquet for Jesus at his house, and a large crowd of tax collectors and others came and were eating with them" (Luke 5:29 NIV).

Matthew wasn't content just to follow Jesus himself. He wanted all of his friends to experience the same joy and peace and life-changing salvation that he had found in Jesus.

So he threw this great banquet at his house and invited all his friends to come meet Jesus. Don't forget who Matthew's friends were! They were the offscouring of Jewish society. They were the "untouchables" of Israel. They were other tax collectors as well as prostitutes and criminals and drunks and recalcitrant Jews, all gathered together under one roof!

If we use our imagination a little, at some point, Matthew rose to speak. Maybe he told a few "tax collector" jokes to begin with, and then he said, "You know, something happened to me a few days ago that I want to tell you about, because it radically changed my life.

"A few days ago, I committed my life to Jesus as my Messiah and Lord. And He's here tonight. I want you to listen to Him for a few minutes."

As Jesus rose to speak, I'm sure all those in the room braced themselves, expecting to hear more of the same rejection and deprecation that the Jewish rabbis had been hurling at them for years. Instead, Jesus told them about how much God loved them, about how much God wanted to forgive them, and about the newness of life that God wanted to give them.

It's interesting that the Bible never tells us how many of these outcasts from Jewish society made decisions for

Jesus Christ that night—but I'll bet you that when we get to heaven, we're going to be shocked at how many people from Matthew's dinner we'll see there!

As you might expect, the Jewish rabbis were not thrilled about this dinner or about the fact that Jesus was there. Luke 5:30 says, "But the Pharisees and the teachers of the law who belonged to their sect complained to His [Jesus'] disciples, 'Why do you eat and drink with tax collectors and sinners?'" (NIV). Their point was: "How can Jesus call Himself a holy Man of God and still rub shoulders and even eat dinner with scum like this?"

"Jesus answered them, 'It is not the healthy who need a doctor, but the sick. I have not come to call the righteous, but sinners to repentance'" (Luke 5:31–32 NIV).

Jesus drew on simple human logic to answer the rabbis' question: "Hey, doctors are for sick people, not healthy people. And since I'm a doctor for sinners, it only makes sense that I go where my patients are."

The reality is that, as human beings and members of Adam's race, we're *all* spiritually sick people in the sight of a holy God. Therefore, we *all* need the healing touch of Jesus, the Great Physician.

The tragedy is that the rabbis, in their self-righteous arrogance, considered themselves to be healthy people who needed neither a doctor nor a savior.

If you've never embraced Jesus Christ as your Lord and Savior, let me point out to you that in presenting Himself in this passage as a doctor, Jesus wants to help you better understand exactly what He's offering to do for you if you will simply humble yourself and let Him.

Think for a moment. What do good doctors do? They do three things.

Number one—good doctors really care about people who are sick. They are not interested in our fees; they are interested in us, and they make themselves available to help us, not just during office hours, but whenever we need them.

Number two—good doctors accept us just as we are. They don't send us away to get well before seeing them. No matter how sick we may be when we go to see them, good doctors accept us right where we are and do not condemn us for being sick.

Number three—if we are sick, good doctors are never content to leave us the way they found us. They're committed to healing us, making us well, and making our lives better.

All of this is found in Jesus' offer to each of us in Matthew 11:28:

- **"Come to Me"**—because I'm interested in you.
- **"All you who are weary and heavy laden"**—you don't have to get well first. Just come to Me as you are.
- **"And I will give you rest for your soul"**—I won't leave you the way I found you. I'll heal your sin-sick soul, repair your broken life, and make you into a new person in Christ.

This is what Jesus did for Matthew. It's what He did for hundreds of Matthew's friends that night, and it's what He's offering to do for you if you'll do what any patient must do:

- Admit to yourself and the doctor that you're sick.
- Turn to the doctor for help.
- Surrender yourself fully to the doctor's care.

I hope you'll do that today.

All of this leads us to ask: "**So what**? What difference does anything in Luke chapter 5 make in my life?"

Matthew (Following Jesus Correctly)

Jesus said to Matthew in Luke chapter 5: **"Follow Me!"**

Upon closer examination of the New Testament, we find that this was the consistent invitation that Jesus issued to people.

- To Peter, Andrew, James, and John in Mark chapter 1, Jesus said, **"Follow Me!"**
- To Philip in John chapter 1, Jesus said, **"Follow Me!"**
- To the rich young ruler in Luke chapter 18, Jesus said, **"Follow Me!"**
- In John 10:27, Jesus said, "My sheep hear My voice, and I know them, and they **follow Me**" (NKJV).
- In Mark 10:28, Peter said to Jesus, "We have left everything to **follow You!**" (NIV).
- In Matthew 16:24, Jesus said, "If anyone wishes to come after Me, let him deny himself, and take up his cross, and **follow Me**" (NKJV).

You may say, "Okay, Lon—you've made your point. It's clear that Jesus is calling people to **"Follow Him,"** but where? How? In what?

That's a great question. So let's answer it!
Jesus calls us to **"follow Him"** into three things.
First, **into a life of biblical obedience.**

- 1 Samuel 15:22: "Does the Lord delight in burnt offerings and sacrifices as much as in obeying the Lord? To obey is better than sacrifice" (NIV).
- Luke 6:46: "Why do you call me, 'Lord, Lord,' and do not do what I say?" (NIV).

"Following Jesus" means that we commit ourselves to living in biblical obedience regardless of the cost. This doesn't mean we always get it right every day, but that we're always *trying* to get it right.

Second, **into a life of godly service to Jesus.** Throughout the New Testament, the terms "follower of Jesus" and "servant of Jesus" are joined at the hip.

- Paul called himself "a *servant* of Jesus Christ" (Romans 1:1).
- James called himself "a *servant* of Jesus Christ" (James 1:1).
- Simon Peter called himself "a *servant* of Jesus Christ" (2 Peter 1:1).

- Jude called himself "a *servant* of Jesus Christ" (Jude 1:1).
- John said that he was "God's *servant*" (Revelation 1:1).

You might say, "But Lon, God didn't call me to serve him full-time and vocationally in the ministry like Peter, James, John, and Paul."

The answer is: **"Oh, yes, He did!"**

As followers of Jesus, God calls every one of us to serve Jesus full time. He calls us to define our lives as "servants of Jesus Christ." He calls on us to derive our meaning in life from being "servants of Jesus," whether we ever get any salary from it or not.

The Bible says to us as Christ-followers, "Whatever you do, do it heartily, as to the Lord and not to men, knowing that ... you serve the Lord Christ" (Colossians 3:23–24 NKJV).

So whether you are a minister, a plumber, a stay-at-home mom—a butcher, a baker, or a candlestick maker—you are to carry out your tasks unto the Lord as His servant.

Third, **into a life of telling other people about the Lord Jesus and His offer of salvation.**

In Mark 1:17, Jesus said to Peter and Andrew, "Follow Me, and I will make you become fishers of men" (NKJV).

Isn't this precisely what happened with Matthew? As soon as he decided to follow Jesus, the very next thing he did was invite all of his friends over to meet Him for themselves. And, to this very day, this is Jesus' plan for you and me and every believer in Him. As Jesus said in Acts 1:8, "You will be my witnesses" (NIV).

So, let's summarize. As Christians, Jesus calls us to "Come, follow Him…"

1. Into a life of *biblical obedience.*
2. Into a life of *godly service to Christ.*
3. Into a life of *telling people everywhere about God's offer of salvation that is found in Jesus' work on the cross for us.*

Following Jesus correctly is a radical thing. It's not a Band-Aid treatment that you stick on top of your existing lifestyle. It's a radical surgery that redefines your life and your lifestyle forever—into a Christocentric life instead of an egocentric life.

You may keep the same job, house, hobby, car, golf clubs, and workout routine, but these things are no longer the central focus of your life—**Jesus is!**

You say, "But Lon, I have three objections to this."

Objection #1: "How about the problems that this kind of radical walk with Christ will produce in my family?"

Well, being Jewish, I can totally relate to this!

Jesus said in Matthew 10:37–38, "Anyone who loves their father or mother more than me is not worthy of me; anyone who loves their son or daughter more than me is not worthy of me. Whoever does not take up their cross and follow me is not worthy of me" (NIV).

To follow Jesus correctly means that you must decide whom you love more—Him or your family.

Objection #2: "How about all the creature comforts I may have to give up if I follow Christ as radically as you say I should?"

This is one of the issues Matthew had to deal with. Remember that, as a tax collector, Matthew was a wealthy man. He had plenty of money to throw a huge party for Jesus and a big enough house to hold hundreds of guests. So when Jesus said to Matthew, "Follow Me," He was asking Matthew to turn his back on all of it—to give up his lavish lifestyle and to let Jesus redefine his whole life.

Matthew valued Jesus so much that he did it without hesitation. He left everything behind and followed Jesus, and this is precisely the kind of response that the Risen, Living Christ wants from each one of us.

Jesus said in Matthew 6:24, "No one can serve two masters. ... You cannot serve both God and money" (NIV).

To follow Jesus correctly, you must decide once and for all which master you're serving.

Objection #3: "What if I want to keep hanging on to some of my old lifestyle? What if I agree to follow Jesus 95 percent of the time?"

A divided heart like this is a real problem.

Jesus said in Luke 9:62, "No one who puts a hand to the plow and looks back is fit for service in the kingdom of God" (NIV).

I love the story in the Old Testament where the prophet Elijah called Elisha to follow him and serve God.

Elisha was a farmer, and he was out in the field plowing when Elijah came up to him and delivered this call from God.

See what Elisha did as recorded in 1 Kings 19:21: "So Elisha left him and went back. He took his yoke of oxen and slaughtered them. He burned the plowing equipment to cook the meat and gave it to the people, and they ate. Then he set out to follow Elijah and became his attendant" (NIV).

What was Elisha really telling all his friends by "burning his plowing equipment and killing his oxen"? He was telling them that he had decided to follow Jesus—regardless of the cost—and that going back to his former life was simply not one of the options, ever!

So, my friend, to follow Jesus correctly, you too must "burn the plowing equipment and slaughter the oxen" of your previous life.

Let's conclude.

It is my firm belief that one of the greatest scourges we face today in American Christianity is all of the people who *claim* to be followers of Jesus, but follow Him incorrectly:

- *Without* a passion for biblical obedience.
- *Without* being servants of Christ but still being servants of themselves.
- *Without* being bold/outspoken witnesses for Jesus and His gospel.

Truthfully, it would be much better for Christianity in America if we had fewer people *claiming* to be followers of Christ, so long as they all followed Him *correctly*.

As Jim Elliott, missionary to the Auca Indians who killed him in 1956, said, "He is no fool who gives up what he cannot keep to gain what he cannot lose."

This is my challenge to us today, that by the power of the Holy Spirit, we rise up like Matthew and Elisha and Jim Elliott and follow Jesus correctly for the glory of our God.

5

The Rich Man and Lazarus (The Afterlife)

ONE OF THE most enduring hits of rock guitarist Eric Claption is his 1992 song titled, "Tears in Heaven."

Clapton wrote this song after the tragic death of his four-year-old son, who accidentally fell through a window and plunged to his death.

In his song, Clapton asks a series of doleful questions:

- "Would you know my name if I saw you in heaven?"
- "Would it be the same if I saw you in heaven?"
- "Would you hold my hand if I saw you in heaven?
- "Would you help me stand if I saw you in heaven?"

At some point, I think every thinking person alive wonders what's on the other side of the grave—what the afterlife really looks like.

This is what we want to talk about here in Chapter 5.

The passage for this chapter is found in the gospel according to Luke, chapter 16.

But before we start, allow me to point out that Jesus never calls this story a parable. Moreover, Jesus uses the beggar's name in the story—something he does in none of His parables in the Bible. Therefore, many commentators (and I agree with them) consider this passage in Luke 16 to be a real-life story about two real-life people. But even if it is a parable, it doesn't change the theological truths Jesus teaches in it about the afterlife.

"There was a certain rich man who was clothed in purple and fine linen and fared sumptuously every day. But there was a certain beggar named Lazarus, full of sores, who was laid at his gate, desiring to be fed with the crumbs which fell from the rich man's table. *[The clear implication here is that Lazarus never got any of these crumbs.]* Moreover the dogs came and licked his sores. So it was that the beggar died, and was carried by the angels to Abraham's bosom" (Luke 16:19–22a NKJV).

Now Lazarus most likely died on the street, right in front of the rich man's house. He probably had no funeral service, casket, or gravestone—but what a bunch of pallbearers he had: the very angels of heaven! They came and

The Rich Man and Lazarus (The Afterlife)

carried him to "Abraham's bosom," which in Jesus' time was a common Jewish expression for heaven.

So Lazarus died and ended up in heaven—but what about the rich man?

"The rich man also died and was buried. In Hades…" (Luke 16:22b–23a NIV).

The rich man died and no doubt had a big funeral service; but, in contrast to Lazarus, the Bible says the rich man suddenly found himself in Hades.

"In Hades, where he was in torment, he looked up and saw Abraham far away, with Lazarus by his side" (Luke 16:23 NIV).

What occured next was one of the most amazing and important conversations ever recorded.

"So he called to him, 'Father Abraham, have pity on me and send Lazarus to dip the tip of his finger in water and cool my tongue, because I am in agony in this fire'" (Luke 16:24 NIV).

Maybe for the first time in his life, the rich man humbled himself and begged for mercy from God.

This is a good place for us to stop and ask: "Did this rich man end up in hell because he was rich?" The answer is absolutely not! Abraham was one of the richest people on earth in his day, and yet he was clearly in heaven.

The reason this rich man ended up in hell was because his money had made him so arrogant and smug that he'd never humbled himself, admitted he was a sinner, and turned to God for mercy before he died here on earth.

"But Abraham replied, 'Son, remember that in your lifetime you received your good things, while Lazarus received bad things, but now he is comforted here and you are in agony. And besides all this, between us and you a great chasm has been set in place, so that those who want to go from here to you cannot, nor can anyone cross over from there to us'" (Luke 16:25–26 NIV).

Abraham's response was stark and shocking. He said, "You had your chance on earth to appeal to God for mercy, but you spurned it. There's a great chasm that's fixed between you in hell and us in heaven. Sadly, all of us in heaven see what's happening to you in hell, and we would *like* to come and help you, but I'm so sorry—it's simply not permitted."

"He answered, 'Then I beg you, father, send Lazarus to my family, for I have five brothers. Let him warn them, so that they will not also come to this place of torment.' Abraham replied, 'They have Moses and the Prophets; let them listen to them'" (Luke 16:27–29 NIV).

The Rich Man and Lazarus (The Afterlife)

To understand what Abraham was saying here, we must understand that the Jews of Jesus' day divided the Old Testament into two parts:

- **The Torah**—the first five books of the Bible, written by Moses.
- **The remainder of the Old Testament**—written by various prophets.

So when Abraham said, "They have Moses and the Prophets," he was saying, "They have the written Word of God, in which is recorded God's offer of salvation. They need to humble themselves before the authority of God's Word and call on God for mercy as it says—and they'll get it!"

"'No, father Abraham,' [said the rich man], 'but if someone from the dead goes to them, they will repent.' He [Abraham] said to him, 'If they do not listen to Moses and the Prophets, they will not be convinced even if someone rises from the dead'" (Luke 16:30–31 NIV).

Abraham said to the rich man, "You still don't get it, do you? It's all about the condition of the heart. If your brothers' hearts are tender toward God, and ready to do business with Him, they will hear God's voice in the words of the Bible, calling them to repent, and they'll respond; but if their hearts are hard toward God, somebody could even rise from the dead and they'd still spurn God."

I must remind you that somebody *did* rise from the dead, and lots of people still refused to believe, just as Abraham predicted.

It is here that the narrative ends:

- With Lazarus securely in heaven—forever.
- With the rich man tragically in hell—forever.
- And with the rich man's five brothers back on earth needing to humble themselves, to believe God's written Word, and to cry out to the Lord Jesus Christ for mercy to avoid the same fate as their brother.

All this leads to our key question: "**So what?**"

In her epic book titled *On Death and Dying*, Dr. Elisabeth Kubler-Ross—who investigated twenty thousand "near death experiences"—wrote: "Up until I did these studies, I had absolutely no belief in an afterlife. … The data, however, has convinced me and now … I have no shadow of a doubt that there is life after death."

The Rich Man and Lazarus (The Afterlife)

Lots of other doctors disagree. Dr. Dorothy Whipple (in *Johns Hopkins Magazine*): "When you die, you don't land anywhere. You just blow out the candle."

So who's right? Is there an afterlife or not? And if so, what exactly does it look like?

The only person who can answer this is Jesus. He's Almighty God wrapped in human flesh. He's the owner and sole proprietor of the afterlife. And He's the one who's been there and back!

And here in Luke 16, Jesus told us that there is indeed an afterlife. Moreover, here we have Jesus' longest and most detailed description in the Bible about what the afterlife holds for us. He tells us four important facts.

Fact #1: In the afterlife, people keep their same identity as on earth. Lazarus was still Lazarus. The rich man was still the rich man. In fact, 2,000 years later, Abraham was still Abraham. In the same way, after you and I die, you're still going to be you and I'm still going to be me *for all eternity*.

Fact #2: In the afterlife, people keep their memory, their reasoning, and their senses. Abraham, Lazarus, and the rich man were all fully conscious, fully awake, and fully aware. They could see, speak, and hear. They could think logically. The rich man could remember his brothers back on earth and even tried to negotiate for them. Unlike Abraham and Lazarus, who were free of pain in heaven, the rich man experienced torment and grief.

Fact #3: In the afterlife, there are only two options of where a person will spend eternity:

- Heaven, which the Bible depicts as a wonderful place.
- Hell, which the Bible depicts as a terrible place.

I have heard people say, as I am sure many of you have, "Well, if I do go to hell, at least I'll have all of my friends there, and we'll party on for eternity."

Please notice that this isn't at all how Jesus described hell. Here in Luke 16, Jesus described it as a "place of fire." Four times, in describing hell, He used the words "torment" and "agony." This rich man certainly wasn't having a blast in hell, was he? All he wanted was to get out of there. *But he couldn't!*

And that brings us to the final and (for many people) most tragic fact about the afterlife.

Fact #4: In the afterlife, the Bible says that people's eternal destinies are "fixed." Their eternal destinies are

The Rich Man and Lazarus (The Afterlife)

set in concrete forever. People who're in heaven (like Abraham and Lazarus) are in heaven *forever*. People who're in hell (like the rich man) are in hell *forever*.

We must understand that when it comes to those people who leave this world without faith in Jesus, and who therefore end up in hell, God withdraws from them His offer of mercy through Jesus' work on the cross.

It's an offer that they spurned in their arrogance and stubbornness while on earth, and now, in hell, the offer is retracted—*forever*.

Of course, when people spurn Jesus on earth and end up in hell, and they experience its horrors for themselves, just like the rich man, they're now frantic about appealing to God for mercy, but the offer has been retracted.

In Dante's "Inferno," the inscription over the Gate of Hell reads: "Through me one enters the sorrowful city. Through me one enters into eternal pain. ... I endure eternally. All hope abandon, ye who enter here."

In truth, hell is far worse than any words can explain. And the worst part of all is that, for those who end up there, it is eternal.

Above every other reason, this is why Jesus came and gave His life on the cross for you and me. It was because He knew the awful reality of hell!

Do you really think Jesus would have died such a gruesome death to save us from a myth? If the worst thing that was going to happen to us after we die is that we're going to be "blown out like a candle," do you really think Jesus would have gone to the cross to save us from that?

If you have never embraced Jesus as your Savior from hell, have never placed your full trust in His shed blood on the cross as your only payment for your sin before a holy God and as your only hope of escape from hell and entry into heaven, then I beg you to take heed of the truth of the Bible and do so today. Right now!

For us as followers of Jesus, the "**So what?**" for us is that our witnessing and evangelism need to get a fresh glimpse of the reality of hell!

In a new and compelling way, we need to realize that when we offer Jesus to people, we're not just offering them a better way to live their earthly lives—to have more peace of mind and more power over their sinful lusts and more closeness to God here on earth. We are indeed offering them these things, but the stakes are astronomically higher than that. The stakes are eternity in heaven vs. eternity in hell.

As followers of Jesus, if realizing this doesn't kindle a passion in us for lost people, then I don't know what will,

The Rich Man and Lazarus (The Afterlife)

In Acts 20:26-27, the Apostle Paul said, "Therefore, I declare to you today that I am innocent of the blood of any of you. For I have not hesitated to proclaim to you the whole will of God" (NIV).

Paul was talking about Ezekiel 33:7-9, where the Lord said, "I have made you a watchman for the house of Israel; therefore you shall hear a word from My mouth and warn them for Me. When I say to the wicked, 'O wicked man, you shall surely die!' and you do not speak out to warn the wicked man from his way, that wicked man shall die in his iniquity; but his blood I will require at your hand. Nevertheless if you warn the wicked to turn from his way, and he does not turn from his way, he shall die for his iniquity; but you have delivered your soul" (NKJV).

Paul was saying to the Ephesians in Acts 20, "I am innocent of all men's blood, because I never let anybody pass me by without telling them the Gospel message about heaven, hell, and salvation in Jesus."

With God's help—as much as humanly possible—I don't want *anybody* to be in hell who might look up at me in heaven and say, "You mean you lived next door to me, you worked in the cubicle next to me, you had me standing on your front porch delivering a package—and you never told me to stay out of this horrid place?"

You might say, "Lon, I hear what you're saying, but I have two objections."

Objection #1: "I object to your putting this kind of guilt and pressure on me. I mean, even if I never open my mouth, the 'elect' will still get saved anyway—right?"

If you're talking about the doctrines of unconditional election and irresistible grace—the belief that God elects certain people to be saved and gives them grace so that they must get saved—and doesn't give that grace to other people so that they can't be saved—sorry, but I don't buy it!

Just look at these verses of Scripture.

"And the Spirit and the bride say, 'Come!' And let him who hears say, 'Come!' And let him who thirsts come. *Whoever* desires, let him take of the water of life freely" (Revelation 22:17 NKJV).

"This is good, and pleases God our Savior, who wants *all people* to be saved and to come to the knowledge of the truth" (1 Timothy 2:3–4 NIV).

Jesus said, "And I, if I am lifted up from the earth [on the cross], will draw *all peoples* to Myself" (John 12:32 NKJV).

The Rich Man and Lazarus (The Afterlife)

Besides—whether you're a Calvinist, an Arminian, or anything in between—the Great Commission still reads: "Go ye into *all* the world and preach the gospel to *every* creature" (Mark 16:15 KJV).

The Bible is saying, "Don't worry about who's elect and who's not elect—just get out there and preach the Gospel!"

As followers of Jesus, God forbid that we should ever use *any* understanding we might have of the doctrine of election as an excuse for evangelistic apathy and witnessing cowardice!

Objection #2: "Are you saying that we should be rude and insist on sharing Jesus, even in situations where to do so would be patently offensive?"

Of course, we must be sensitive to those moments when the Holy Spirit is opening the door for us to share Christ and when He is not.

But, once again, too many Christians hide behind this and use it as a way out of *ever* sharing Christ at all.

"*Always be ready* [anxious] to give a defense to everyone who asks you a reason for the hope that is in you" (1 Peter 3:15 NKJV).

The Bible is saying, "As Christians, be like a loaded spring, always ready to go off—be always 'chomping at the bit' to share Christ with everyone you meet. And try to do so, unless the Holy Spirit expressly calls you off."

So the question is: "How many of us walk out the door every morning actively wanting and hoping and planning to share Jesus with people?"

This is precisely how the early church lived, and it's precisely how God wants us to live today.

In conclusion, not every message in the Bible is a happy one. There are some very tough messages in the Bible, and this one from Luke 16 is certainly one of them: *People who fail to accept Christ on earth spend eternity in hell without remedy.*

My grandparents were both 100 percent Jewish. I shared Jesus with them at least six times, and they refused to believe in Jesus all six times. Unless they changed their minds in their last hours, the Bible says that they're in hell today.

Now, I can refuse to believe this if I want; because this makes me sad, I can pretend it's not true—but as followers of Jesus, we must not allow ourselves to live in this kind of theological denial.

The UPS person at the door; the cashier at the grocery store; our neighbors, friends, coworkers, and relatives—when we look in their faces, we *must* remember that

The Rich Man and Lazarus (The Afterlife)

apart from faith in the Lord Jesus, they're going to spend eternity in hell.

It's our duty and our privilege to tell them "the whole counsel of God" so that they may have a chance to be saved—just like the Apostle Paul and the early church did—but remember, this kind of evangelistic passion and fervor will come only when we decide to believe every piece of what the living, risen Son of God has told us in the Bible about the afterlife.

May God help us do so!

6

Legion (Valuing People)

A SURVEY DONE in 2016 by the Pew Research Center focused on Americans who've switched religions. But the most interesting item in this survey found that 16 percent of those surveyed (almost one out of every six Americans) have switched from Catholicism or Protestantism to "no religion at all."

When pollsters asked these "no religion" people why they quit going to church, almost all of them gave one of three answers:

1. Religious people are too hypocritical and judgmental of others.
2. Churches focus too much on rules.
3. Church leaders focus too much on accumulating power and money.

As I thought about this, it occurred to me that in all of these three answers, people are really saying the very same thing: religious people and churches and church leaders don't really care or value people. They value dogma and rules, power and money, but they don't really care about people.

Whether this is really true of us as Christians is not the point. The point is that this is how one out of six Americans sees us at Christians.

And this is a serious problem, because, if we've given the impression to one out of six Americans that God's heart is all about power, money, and legalistic dogma, then our chances of reaching them for Christ are very slim indeed.

This is what we want to talk about as we continue meeting the people Jesus met: the importance and the value that God places on people.

Mark 5:1: "Then they [Jesus and His disciples] came to the other side of the sea, to the country of the Gadarenes. And when He had come out of the boat, immediately there met Him out of the tombs a man with a unclean spirit" (NKJV).

The lake referred to here is the Sea of Galilee. Jesus and His disciples had taken a small boat from the northwest side of sea at the city of Capernaum to the village of Judea on the east side of the Sea of Galilee.

Legion (Valuing People)

At this site today, there are the remnants of a church built by Helena, the mother of Emperor Constantine, during her pilgrimage through the Holy Land in 325–326 AD. In the hills just above this church are hundreds of natural caves that were used as tombs in the time of Jesus. It was from one of these caves that this demon-possessed man came out to meet Jesus.

Let's remember what Jesus had done prior to this:

1. First, He demonstrated His power over sickness and disease in Mark 1 and 2.
2. Second, He demonstrated His power over death in Luke 7.
3. Third, He demonstrated His power over the forces of nature in Mark 4.

Now, here in Mark 5, Jesus is about to demonstrate His power over the devil and his kingdom of demons.

Many people in our world today believe that no educated person really thinks that the devil or his demons exist. They believe that when the Bible talks about the devil and demons, it's all just a symbol for evil in the world.

But the Bible categorically declares that the devil Satan is a real angelic being who led a revolt against God in the heavenly places before the world was created, and that demons were fellow angels who followed him. As a result, God cast the devil and his demons out of heaven and down to this earth, where they are free to roam until their final destruction in the Lake of Fire (Revelation 20).

But make no mistake: the Bible clearly states that, here on earth, God still has absolute power and authority over Satan and his demons, as we are about to witness in Mark 5.

I totally believe this. And if you say that you believe the Bible is the inspired, inerrant Word of God, then you must believe it, too.

Mark 5:3–5: "This man lived in the tombs, and no one could bind him anymore, not even with a chain. For he had often been chained hand and foot, but he tore the chains apart and broke the irons on his feet. No one was strong enough to subdue him. Night and day among the tombs and in the hills he would cry out and cut himself with stones" (NIV).

How sad is this? What a poor and pitiful fella!

Mark 5:6–8: "When he saw Jesus from a distance, he ran and fell on his knees in front of him. He shouted at

Legion (Valuing People)

the top of his voice, 'What do you want with me, Jesus, Son of the Most High God? In God's name don't torture me!' For Jesus had said to him, 'Come out of this man, you impure spirit!'" (NIV).

Please notice the great contrast here. No human power or authority could tame these demons, but they fell down powerless at the feet of Jesus, declaring Him to be the "Son of the Most High God."

While on the way over the Sea of Galilee to meet this man, the disciples had asked the question: "Who can this be, that even the wind and the sea obey him!" (Mark 4:41 NKJV). And now the demons have answered the question for them: "He is the Son of the Most High God."

Mark 5:9: "Then He [Jesus] asked him [the demon], 'What is your name?' And he answered, saying, 'My name is Legion; for we are many'" (NKJV).

A Roman legion consisted of 6,000 foot soldiers and 1,000 cavalry plus support troops. So there must have been a bunch of demons inside this poor tormented man.

Mark 5:10–13: "And he [Legion] begged Jesus again and again not to send them out of the area. A large herd of pigs was feeding on the nearby hillside. The demons begged Jesus, 'Send us among the pigs; allow us to go into them.' He gave them permission, and the impure spirits came out and went into the pigs" (NIV).

We learn from Mark 5:14 that these pigs were not wild but domesticated; people were "tending" them.

I think most of us know that pigs are not kosher. So what in the world were these Jewish people over there doing—*raising pigs*?

The answer is that these weren't Jewish people; the east side of the Sea of Galilee (where Jesus and His disciples were in Mark 5) was populated by Gentiles. In fact, we also know that on the east and south sides of the Sea of Galilee at this time, there was a ten-city Gentile confederation known as the Decapolis. Furthermore, we also know that raising pigs was a major industry for them, just as the Bible says.

Mark 5:13: "The herd, about two thousand in number, rushed down the steep bank into the lake and were drowned" (NIV).

This represented a *gigantic* financial loss for people Gedara, which explains what happened next.

Mark 5:14–16: "Those tending the pigs ran off and reported this in the town and countryside, and the people went out to see what had happened. When they came to Jesus, they saw the man who had been possessed by the

Legion (Valuing People)

legion of demons, sitting there, dressed and in his right mind; and they were afraid. Those who had seen it told the people what had happened to the demon-possessed man—and told about the pigs as well" (NIV).

Let's stop for a moment and think about the situation that the townspeople found themselves in. On the one hand, you've got the demoniac whose pathetic life had been redeemed, restored, and reclaimed. On the other hand you've got 2,000 pigs floating in the sea of Galilee like corks, representing a huge sum of money that's been lost.

And just how did the townspeople react?

Mark 5:17: "Then the people began to plead with Jesus to leave their region" (NIV).

They said to Jesus: "Hey, pal. We don't know who you are or where you came from. But we want you to get in that little boat and go right back to wherever you came from before you end up costing us more pigs!"

I'm sure there must have been a lot of sick people back in their town. Jesus could have helped them just as he had helped Legion. But instead of caring about how many human lives Jesus might have been able to heal and restore and reclaim if He were invited to stay on with them, what these townsfolk cared most about is how many more pigs they might lose.

Mark 5:18–19: "And when He got into the boat, he who had been demon-possessed begged Him that he might be with Him. However, Jesus did not permit him, but said to him, 'Go home to your friends, and tell them what great things the Lord has done for you, and how He has had compassion on you'" (NKJV).

It occurs to me that Jesus could have said to him, "You're right, Legion. These folks have rejected you all of your life, and now they've rejected Me, too. C'mon, get in the boat, and let's wash our hands of these people for good."

But in spite of their rejection of Him, Jesus loved and valued these people so much that He told Legion to stay there, to become a traveling evangelist, and to keep trying to reach them for Christ.

Mark 5:20: "And he departed and began to proclaim in Decapolis all that Jesus had done for him; and all marveled [at his story]" (NKJV).

Here we have the first great outdoor evangelist in history. Before Wesley, Moody, Luis Palau, or Billy Graham, there was our friend Legion!

Legion (Valuing People)

So let's ask our most important question now: "**So what?**"

I believe that the most tragic part of this story is the value system we see in the people of Gedara: that they valued pigs more than people.

The rabbis in Jesus' day had the very same problem. But, for the rabbis, it wasn't pigs they valued more than people—it was their rules and traditions and positions of power. But it's still the same disease that the people of Gedara had.

Matthew 12:9–10: "He [Jesus] went into their synagogue, and a man with a shriveled hand was there. Looking for a reason to bring charges against Jesus, they [the rabbis] asked him, 'Is it lawful to heal on the Sabbath?'" (NIV).

We should know that the rabbis at this time had twelve books of rules regarding restrictions on the Sabbath. These rules were unbelievably oppressive:

- A person was allowed to walk only 3,000 feet from home on the Sabbath—any more than that was considered "work."
- A person was not allowed to swat an insect.

- Women were not allowed to look in the mirror at themselves because they might find a gray hair and attempt to pull it out, which would qualify as "work."
- People were not allowed to climb a tree or ride a horse or swim or dance or even spit on the ground—much less heal a sick person.

Certainly, Jesus could have waited until the next day to heal this man. But by healing him on the Sabbath, Jesus wanted to teach the rabbis something very important about God: that people are more important to Him than all the little religious rules.

Matthew 12:11–13: "He [Jesus] said to them, 'If any of you has a sheep and it falls into a pit on the Sabbath, will you not take hold of it and lift it out? How much more valuable is a person than a sheep! Therefore it is lawful to do good on the Sabbath.' Then he said to the man, 'Stretch out your hand.' So he stretched it out and it was completely restored" (NIV).

And remember, Jesus was not violating the Bible *or* breaking the Sabbath. The Bible never forbids healing a person on the Sabbath. What Jesus was breaking was the

Legion (Valuing People)

petty, legalistic rules that had become more important to these rabbis than people.

Matthew 12:14: "But the Pharisees went out and plotted how they might kill Jesus" (NIV).

In both of these stories, Jesus was trying to teach us the very same truth: that above all else, God cares about and values people.

Let's bring all of this forward into the twenty-first century and say that we, as the church of Jesus Christ today, desperately need to be reminded of the biblical truth.

We desperately need to be reminded that Jesus didn't die on the cross for buildings or parking spaces or denominations or offering plates or attendance figures or legalistic church rules or power-hungry pastors.

Jesus died on the cross for **people.**
He died for:

- Men with long hair, earrings, and tattoos.
- Women who are pregnant and unwed with no place to turn.
- People with substance abuse problems.
- People with AIDS.
- People who are struggling with homosexuality.

- Homeless people.
- Children who have been abused.
- Single-parent moms and dads who are struggling to make ends meet.
- Teenagers who are angry and hurt.
- Children who don't know who their father is or why they left their family.

These are people who matter to God!

- People whom Jesus loves.
- People for whom Jesus died.
- People who need Christ.

And the big "**so what**" for us as believers today is this: Are we going to have the value system of the townsfolk in Gedara? Are we going to have the value system of the first-century rabbis? Or are we going to have the value system of the Lord Jesus?

And our churches need to ask: Are we going to define our success by buildings and parking lots and offerings and attendance figures? Or are we going to define our success by how many people's lives we change for eternity through Jesus Christ?

Legion (Valuing People)

Are we going to open our arms to people of every race and creed and background and color and socio-economic condition, even if it gets a little messy or if it presses us out of our comfort zone?

In other words, are we going to be a "hospital for sinners" or a "museum for saints"? Are we going to be a M.A.S.H. unit or a country club?

A few years ago, a young man started showing up at the church where I was serving as senior pastor. He had torn jeans, long hair, multiple earrings, an unshaven face, bloodshot eyes, and body odor. With him was a young lady who had many of the same physical signs of depletion and whose attire would never qualify as "modest," no matter whose definition of that word we were using. Every week, they'd walk right down to the front of the auditorium and sit in the front row.

I later discovered that they both had advanced cases of AIDS that they'd contracted from using dirty needles.

But they were in the auditorium, sitting in the front row, because as death was creeping up them, they were looking for answers.

To make a long story short, one Sunday morning, as I gave a salvation appeal at end of the sermon, they decided to give their lives to Jesus. And as they held hands, the two of them joined with me in praying the sinner's prayer. And they meant business, too!

After that, they never missed a Sunday, always in the front row, Bibles open on their laps, drinking in God's Word like dry sponges.

Less than three months after he accepted Christ, I buried that young man. The young lady went not too long after that.

Here's my question for us today: Do our churches have room for people like this? Do we have open arms and open hearts for people like this? And do you personally have room for them?

Do we carry Gospel tracts with us everywhere we go? And do we stop and give them, along with some money, to panhandlers and homeless people on the street and people asking for money at stoplights? Do we take the time to be nice to delivery men and women, to cashiers, to trash collectors, to utility workers, to people with disabilities, and to all the other people whom the vast majority of Christians simply ignore?

I say the answer to these questions should be absolutely yes! Not to condone their sinful behavior, but to love them in Jesus' name and to see them give their lives to Him. And not because these folks are easy to reach or because they are vitally interested in the Gospel at that moment. But because every one of these people matter to God—so much so that He died on the cross for them.

Caring for people, seeing people come to Christ, and seeing Christ transform their lives just as He did Legion's life—as followers of Jesus, this is our calling, our mandate, our mission for God's glory.

Amen!

7

The Centurion
(Faith That Amazes God)

IT'S A WORD we all use all the time, one that punctuates almost every conversation. It's the word *amazing*.

When we say that something amazes us, we mean (of course) that is surprises us or shocks us.

Here in Chapter 7, the Lord Jesus meets someone who amazes Him—a man whose faith literally shocks Him.

We want to figure out exactly what kind of faith this man had that so impressed Jesus, and then talk about how you and I as believers in Christ can have that same kind of faith.

Luke 7:1: "When Jesus had finished saying all this to the people who were listening, he entered Capernaum" (NIV).

Capernaum was the home base of Jesus' ministry for the last three years of His earthly life. It was a village on the northwest shore of the Sea of Galilee, where Peter was from, and it contained a sizable Jewish population at the time of Jesus.

Luke 7:2–3: "There [in Capernaum] a centurion's servant, whom his master valued highly, was sick and about to die. The centurion heard of Jesus and sent some elders of the Jews to him [Jesus], asking him to come and heal his servant" (NIV).

As Jesus reached the edge of Capernaum, He was greeted by a delegation of Jewish community leaders who came to see Him regarding a local centurion.

A "centurion" was a professional, a career Roman military officer. Centurions (from the Latin word "century") commanded units of around 100 soldiers. They were roughly equivalent to a captain in the U.S. Army today, and they formed the backbone of the Roman army at that time.

Centurions were the only Roman officers to wear silver armor and to have their helmet plumes go from side-to-side (ear to ear) instead of back-to-front as higher-ranking officers had. The reason for these differences was so that soldiers could always spot their centurions quickly in middle of a firefight.

Centurions were renowned for being tough and battle-hardened and even brutal at times to their own men. This explains why one Bible commentator remarked, "The reason the Roman army was so fierce in

The Centurion (Faith That Amazes God)

battle is that they were more afraid of their centurions than they were the enemy."

But the Bible tells us that this particular centurion was not your average centurion in two dramatic ways:

1. The Bible tells us that this centurion was a compassionate man. We know this because of how the Bible tells us how he treated his servant. Verse 2 says, "[He had a servant] whom his master valued highly." In Matthew chapter 8, the Bible tells us this servant was a "little boy." It also tells us that this little boy was paralyzed and in great pain, very possibly suffering from polio. But in Roman society, slaves were considered pieces of property, like livestock. Their masters could buy and sell, beat and kill them at will. No Roman master really cared about a slave, but this Roman centurion did!
2. The Bible tells us that he was also a God-fearing man. Verses 4–5: "When they [the Jewish leaders] came to Jesus, they begged Him earnestly, saying that the one for whom He should do this was deserving, for he loves our nation and has built us a synagogue" (NKJV). Does this strike you as

a little odd? Well, it should! The Jewish people of Jesus' day hated the Romans. They saw them as foreign occupiers of Jewish land, and their hostility toward the Roman army ran deep. Yet here we find Jewish leaders pleading this Roman officer's case before Jesus, because this Roman was different. Notice: he "loves our nation" and he even had his soldiers "build us a synagogue" in Capernaum.

By the way, when archaeologists excavated the ancient city of Capernaum, they found this very synagogue dating to the time of Jesus in the town, just as the Bible says. As I always like to say, "The more they dig out of the ground, the more the Bible proves to be right!"

The point of all this is that this centurion had rejected all the frivolous gods and goddesses of the Roman pantheon and had developed a love for the true and living God—which meant that: (1) he had learned the values of compassion and mercy, even for slaves; and that (2) he had also developed a love for God's people, the Jews. All of this had endeared this centurion to the Jewish people of Capernaum so deeply that they came to

The Centurion (Faith That Amazes God)

the Lord Jesus and said, "You know, Jesus, You should do this for this man."

Luke 7:6–7: "So Jesus went with them [the Jewish leaders]. He was not far from the [centurion's] house when the centurion sent friends to say to him: 'Lord, don't trouble yourself, for I do not deserve to have you come under my roof. That is why I did not even consider myself worthy to come to you" (NIV).

Want to see some faith? Well, just see what the centurion says to Jesus!

Luke 7:7b: "But say the word, and my servant will be healed" (NIV).

When the centurion heard that Jesus was coming to see him personally, he sent a second entourage to Jesus with this message: "Lord, please—as a Gentile, as a Roman soldier who's killed lots of people, and as an occupier of Jewish land—I'm not worthy of Your making a personal trip to my house. Besides, Lord, You and I both know that it really isn't necessary for You to come to my house personally to heal my servant. All You need to do is to speak the word and give the order, and my servant will be healed."

What was the centurion's logic behind what he said? Here it is.

Luke 7:8: "For I myself am a man under authority, with soldiers under me. I tell this one, 'Go,' and he goes; and that one, 'Come,' and he comes, I say to my servant, 'Do this,' and he does it" (NIV).

In essence, what the centurion said to Jesus was this: "As a Roman military officer, I am a man with authority, and I understand how it works. As a man with authority, my personal presence somewhere isn't necessary for me to get something done. I just speak the word and give the order, and because I have authority, my wishes are carried out!"

And the centurion continued: "And so, Jesus, because You are a man with authority, all the authority in the universe, Your personal presence isn't necessary at my house. Just speak the word and give the order, and some angel or sepaph or cherub or other heavenly being will come to my house and carry out Your wishes, Lord."

Luke 7:9: "When Jesus heard this, he was *amazed* at him, and turning to the crowd following him, he said, 'I tell you, I have not found such great faith even in Israel'" (NIV).

This Greek word *thaumazo* ("to be amazed") is used a number of times in the New Testament referring to Jesus. However, this is the only time it is used positively. Many

The Centurion (Faith That Amazes God)

times, the Bible says that Jesus was amazed at people's unbelief or hardness of heart or lack of compassion for their fellow man. But here in Luke 7 (and its synoptic parallels) is the only time where the Bible says that Jesus was *amazed* at someone in a good way,

And what "amazed" Jesus here was the faith of this centurion. Here was a man—a Gentile Roman soldier—who viewed all the issues of his life through the lens of Jesus' unlimited power and boundless authority as the Son of God over every detail of the universe.

And the fact that this Gentile had such a deep and thorough understanding of who Jesus really was—when Jesus' own Jewish people didn't—well, this *"amazed"* the Lord Jesus.

Luke 7:10: "Then the men who had been sent returned to his [the centurion's] house and found the servant well" (NIV).

I love the fact that the Lord Jesus took advantage of this platform that the centurion's faith created. He stopped right where He was and never did continue on to the centurion's house. And yet when the centurion's friends returned home, they found the servant completely healed!

All this leads to our key question: **"So what?"**

I am convinced that God *loves* everybody the same, but that He *likes* some people more than He does others!

For example, in Psalms, God called Abraham "my friend." In Genesis, God called David the "apple of His eye"; and in 1 Samuel 13:14, He called David "a man after God's own heart."

In Exodus 33:11, the Bible says that God spoke to Moses "face to face, as a man speaks to his friend" (NKJV). And then there were such people as Caleb and Joshua and Deborah and Ruth and Elijah and Daniel and the Apostle Paul. In fact, God *liked* all these folks so much that He recorded their names in the Holy Bible for everyone to know about them for all eternity.

And the reason God "liked" the people so much is because they saw the world and everything in it *exactly* the way this centurion did.

They saw all of life, every obstacle and problem, and every impossible-looking situation they faced through the lens of God's unlimited power and boundless authority over every detail in the cosmos.

To put it another way, when they encountered what seemed to be even impossible looking obstacles, they refused to limit God, because they understood who He

The Centurion (Faith That Amazes God)

is. They understood His massive power and unrestricted authority over every inch of the universe.

They came right up to those obstacles:

- Like Abraham did with the birth of Isaac
- Like Moses did at the Red Sea
- Like David did with Goliath
- Like Ruth did in going with Naomi
- Like Joshua did at the Jordan River and Jericho
- Like Esther did in going to see the king
- Like Paul did his whole Christian life
- Like this centurion did with his servant's illness

And they trusted God to remove those obstacles right on schedule, in keeping with God's divine plan and sovereign will for the universe, by the supernatural exercise of His awesome power and boundless authority—*plus nothing*!

In other words, the only limiting factor that these folks ever placed on God was His own sovereign will for their lives and His perfect plan for the universe.

Never did they limit God with their puny human logic. Never did they limit God with their puny human understanding. Never did they limit God with their puny human doubts.

Their outlook on everything was childishly simple: "If God decides not to do something for or with me, the only reason should be because He *chooses* not to do it in His own sovereign will, not because I robbed Him of the opportunity to do it and limited Him through my sinful unbelief, doubt, or mental limits I placed on His power."

So you ask, what difference does all this make for me as a follower of Jesus Christ today?

Here's the answer: If there is a single mistake that I see most followers of Jesus make in the world today, it's that they limit God!

So many of us make the same mistake the Israelites in the wilderness made: "Again and again they [the Israelites] tempted God, and limited the Holy One of Israel. They did not remember His power: the day when He redeemed them from the enemy, when He worked His signs in Egypt" (Psalm 78:41–43 NKJV).

But we dare not do this; we dare not forget who our God is.

Over and over, the Bible tells us that we have an omnipotent, omniscient, omnipresent, all-powerful God who is sovereign over every atom in the universe:

The Centurion (Faith That Amazes God)

- Ephesians 3:20: "Now to Him who is able to do exceedingly abundantly above all that we ask or think, according to his power that works in us" (NKJV).
- Luke 1:37: "For with God nothing will be impossible" (NKJV).
- Genesis 18:14: "Is anything too hard for the Lord?" (NKJV).
- Jeremiah 32:27: "I am the Lord, the God of all flesh. Is anything too hard for Me?" (NKJV).
- Matthew 19:26: "Jesus ... said to them, 'With men this is impossible, but with God all things are possible'" (NKJV).
- Luke 18:27: "Jesus replied, 'What is impossible with man is possible with God'" (NIV).

This is how every one of these folks we just mentioned saw God (Abraham, Moses, David, Esther, Ruth, the Apostle Paul). And because they saw God this way, it changed how they saw their world. It changed how they approached their problems, obstacles, and challenges in life.

And as followers of Jesus Christ today, if we will learn to see God in the same way all these folks learned to see God—as the almighty, sovereign, omnipotent, omniscient Being that He truly is—it will forever change how we approach our problems and obstacles and crises in life.

It will result in our never placing artificial human limits on what God will and won't do—or on what God can and can't do—for us.

It will cause us to take God's invitation seriously when He says to us, "Call to Me, and I will answer you, and show you great and mighty things, which you do not know" (Jeremiah 33:3 NKJV).

My oldest son James attended the U.S. Naval Academy and then went on to medical school and became a Navy doctor in anesthesia. He finished his residency at Bethesda Naval Hospital (now Walter Reed Hospital) in the Washington, DC, area in July 2007. The Navy then asked him to do a one-year fellowship in pediatrics at Boston Children's Hospital.

At the time, he had Brenda's and my only two young grandchildren, and to be away from them for a year was something we did not relish.

But this was a great opportunity, and the deal he made with the Navy was that after a year in Boston, he

The Centurion (Faith That Amazes God)

would be reassigned to Bethesda Naval and would be close to Brenda and me again.

But in January 2008, the Naval officer in charge of assigning locations for all of the Navy's anesthesiologists called James and told him that they were going to send him to another duty station altogether. We were all pretty devastated.

So I said, "We need to take God up on Jeremiah 33:3 here."

My son replied that the officer said this decision was 95.5 percent certain, and that he would be receiving orders in the next several weeks, making it 99.5 percent certain.

I said, "James, nothing is certain until Almighty God decides it's certain—so we are going to pray!" And pray we did.

In March, James received his written orders to the alternate duty station. He called me up and said, "Well, Dad, it's over now. I've got my written orders, so you can stop praying."

I said to him, "Oh no, it isn't over! With our God in the picture, it's not over till that moving van pulls up to your door in Boston—and even then, it's not over."

James got so frustrated with me on the phone that he growled, "Humpf—you are SO frustrating!" and quickly ended the conversation.

The truth is that everybody began telling me to stop praying about it and that it was over.

I kept praying, but I changed my prayer.

Before, it was: "Lord, please change the Navy's decision so Brenda and I can be close to our grandchildren."

But now, it was: "Lord, please bare Your mighty arm and reveal Your mighty power and change my son's orders back to DC—and teach my son and his wife and all those involved to *never, ever limit* God."

So let me tell you what happened.

Six weeks later, James called me up and said, "Hey, Dad, you are never going to believe what happened."

I said, "I might. Tell me."

He said, "Well, I got beeped at the hospital in Boston, and I came out of surgery and called the number. It was the officer in charge of assigning all the Navy doctors. He said, 'James, have you made any commitments to housing or other things that you cannot change at that new duty station to which we assigned you?' I told him no. The officer continued, 'Don't make any plans, because I think I have a way to get you back to Washington and

The Centurion (Faith That Amazes God)

Bethesda Naval Hospital.' I answered, 'But sir, I received my written orders weeks ago,' and the officer replied, 'Let me worry about that, OK?'"

And sure enough, several weeks later, James received new written orders sending him back to Bethesda, which is where he served out the entire rest of his twenty-year Naval career!

After James received his new orders, I called and said to him, "James, all of this is awesome. But son, never forget why the Lord did all of this for you. He did it to teach you a really important lesson for the rest of your life—and to pass on to your children. Namely, don't *ever* limit God."

Now, let's add some biblical balance to this: God is not "the genie in the lamp" who's committed to giving whatever we want—nor does he ever claim to be.

But God does claim to be a Being of such boundless power and unlimited authority that He invites us to boldly bring all our problems and challenges to Him. He wants us to lay them at His feet without imposing any limits or pre-conditions on what He will and can do—except those limits He Himself decides to impose.

Of course, we always need to come to God and tell Him that we will humbly accept whatever His will is.

But, in our puny human logic and sinful fleshly unbelief, we must never decide ahead of time what God will or won't do, or what He can or can't do.

Or to put it another way: We must never limit God!

Our attitude should always be that of the great missionary William Carey: "Attempt great things for God—expect great things from God."

You say, "Lon, this is a great goal for us all as true Christians. But how do I get my faith to grow to this size?"

Great question—and the answer is simple.

As followers of Jesus, the Bible never tells us to focus our energies on trying to make our faith greater. The reason for this is that faith is a result, not a cause.

The size of our faith as believers in Jesus is directly proportional to our view of the size of God.

- A big view of God results in a big faith in God.
- A small view of God results in a small faith in God.

The point is this: Don't focus on the size of your faith growing; focus on the size of your God growing.

The Centurion (Faith That Amazes God)

And how do we do this? The Bible tells us in Romans 10:17, "Faith comes by hearing, and hearing by the word of God" (NKJV).

It's by being in the written Word of God—the Bible—that we grow in our understanding, conception, and view of God (His power, authority, majesty, and sovereignty).

As I love to say, we can't build a strong faith on an anemic devotional life.

So *get* in the Word, *stay* in the Word, and *live* in the Word. Let the Bible expand your concept of God until your concept of Him is worthy of Him.

And as you do this, your faith to trust God for great and mighty things will grow into the kind of faith that *amazes* God—just as the centurion's faith did!

8

Thomas (The Exclusivity of Jesus for Salvation)

THE FAMOUS BRITISH novelist George Orwell—author of the books *Animal House* and *1984*—once said, "We have now sunk to such a depth that the restatement of the obvious has become the first duty of intelligent men."

I thought of this quote when I read an article in the paper saying that, according to a nationwide survey, "*Americans of every stripe overwhelmingly believe that all good people go to heaven.*" This is in spite of the fact that the Bible expressly teaches the exact opposite.

And so, in this chapter, in which we'll discuss Jesus meeting His disciple Thomas, I will do what Mr. Orwell said—"to restate the obvious" when it comes to proclaiming Jesus Christ as the exclusive way to possess eternal life and get into heaven.

In John chapter 14, Jesus was talking with His disciples during the Last Supper when the subject of eternal life and heaven came up. And here's what Jesus said: "In My Father's house [meaning heaven] are many mansions; if it were not so, I would have told you. I go to prepare a place for you. And if I go and prepare a place for you, I will come again and receive you to Myself; that where I am, there you may be also" (John 14:2-3 NKJV).

The Bible tells us repeatedly that where Jesus went after His resurrection and ascension (recorded in Acts chapter 1) was to the right hand of God the Father in heaven (Hebrews 1:13, 10:12, etc.). Thus, the promise of Jesus to His followers here in John 14 is that He will receive us into the afterlife and escort us to heaven where He is.

So the first thing that the Bible tells us here, without equivocation, is that there is a real place called heaven where real people can really go after they die on earth.

As a matter of fact, Jesus talked about heaven all the time:

John 6:38: "For I have come down from heaven, not to do My will, but the will of Him who sent Me" (NKJV).

Matthew 5:11-12: "Blessed are you when they revile and persecute you, and say all kinds of evil against you falsely for My sake. Rejoice and be exceedingly glad, for great is your reward in heaven" (NKJV).

Thomas (The Exclusivity of Jesus for Salvation)

And to the thief on the cross, Jesus said, "Assuredly, I say to you, today you will be with Me in Paradise" (Luke 23:43 NKJV).

Catholics would like it to say, "Today you will be in purgatory."

Seventh Day Adventists would like it to say, "Today you will be in soul sleep."

Hindus would like it to say, "Today you will be reincarnated."

Buddhists would like it to say, "Today you will be reabsorbed into the cosmic all."

Atheists would like it to say, "Today you will be blown out like a candle."

Jewish people would like it to say, "Today, your guess is as good as mine as to where you will be."

But Jesus said *none* of these things to the thief on the cross.

And we've all heard people say, "I believe heaven and hell are right here on earth, not places in some fantasy afterlife."

I suppose people are entitled to their own opinions. The only problem with their opinions, however, is that the Risen Son of God, Jesus Christ, says their opinions are all incorrect.

Jesus continued speaking to His disciples in John 14:4: "And where I go you know, and the way you know" (NKJV).

And now, the person Jesus meets in this chapter, the apostle Thomas, entered the scene.

John 14:5: "Thomas said to him, 'Lord, we do not know where You are going, and how can we know the way?'" (NKJV).

This was a reasonable question by Thomas, and Jesus gave him a reasonable answer. It was also a straightforward question, so Jesus gave him a straightforward answer.

"Jesus said to him, 'I am the way, the truth, and the life. No one comes to the Father except through Me'" (John 14:6 NKJV).

Jesus has said this before—that believing in Him is the only way to receive eternal life. For example, John 6:47 said, "Most assuredly, I say to you, he who believes in Me has everlasting life" (NKJV).

But here in John 14:6, Jesus added a most compelling addition to this truth: not only is believing in Him the way a person can attain everlasting life, but believing in Jesus is the *only* way to everlasting life!

Thomas (The Exclusivity of Jesus for Salvation)

Jesus made it crystal clear that sincerity is not the basis upon which God grants people eternal life and lets them into heaven. Nor is religious zeal the basis upon which God does so.

There are sincere and zealous Catholic people who attend mass every day.

There are sincere and zealous Jewish people who keep kosher and go to synagogue every day.

There are sincere and zealous Muslim people who pray five times a day and make their pilgrimages to Mecca.

There are sincere and zealous Hindu people who touch no beef products and bathe in the Ganges.

There are sincere and zealous Baptist people who "don't drink or cuss or smoke or chew or hang around with them which do."

But Jesus declared, without apology, that the *only* basis upon which God grants eternal life and entry into heaven is personal faith in Jesus Christ and active reliance on His blood sacrifice on the cross to pay for our sin in the sight of a Holy God.

This is, in fact, the constant, unbroken, singular, monolithic message of the Bible. Acts 4:12: "Nor is there salvation in any other, for there is *no other name under heaven* given among men by which we must be saved" (NKJV).

In summary, what Jesus said to Thomas here in John 14:6 forms the bedrock of true biblical Christianity—that faith in Jesus and His redeeming work on the cross is the only way to gain eternal life and entry into heaven. Period. End of story.

This now brings us to our most important question: **"So what?"**

Many people in our world today are struggling with this idea that God dispenses eternal life and heaven *only* to those who believe in Jesus.

In fact, a lot of folks struggle with the idea that God grants eternal life and heaven only one way, regardless of what that way may be. They view this notion as intolerant, prejudiced, and just downright mean. Instead, they love the notion that there are many ways to get to heaven and that believing in Jesus is only one of them.

If you're having this struggle, then you've come to the right place. From the Bible, we will settle this issue once and for all.

So first, let's begin by asking the question, "What does God say in the Bible about people who are outside of faith in Jesus?" Look:

Thomas (The Exclusivity of Jesus for Salvation)

- John 3:36: "He who believes in the Son [of God] has everlasting life; and he who does not believe the Son shall not see [everlasting] life, but the wrath of God abides on him" (NKJV).
- John 3:18: "He who believes in Him [Jesus] is not condemned; but he who does not believe is condemned already, because he has not believed in the name of the only begotten Son of God" (NKJV).
- 1 John 5:11-12: "And this is the testimony: that God has given us eternal life, and this life is in His Son [Jesus]. He who has the Son has [eternal] life; he who does not have the Son of God does not have [eternal] life" (NKJV).

How can God say it any clearer than this?

- Acts 4:12: "Nor is there salvation in any other, for there is *no other name under heaven* [not Budda nor Confuscius nor Mohammed nor Joseph Smith nor Mary Baker Eddy nor L. Ron Hubbard nor Rabbi anybody], given among men by which we must be saved" (NKJV).

- And in case there is any doubt remaining, see 2 Thessalonians 1:8–9: "In flaming fire taking vengeance on those who do not know God, and on those who do not obey the gospel of our Lord Jesus Christ. These will be punished with everlasting destruction from the presence of the Lord and from the glory of His power" (NKJV).

Now, you might say, "But Lon, I have four objections to this teaching." OK, let's hear them.

Objection #1: "Isn't the Bible being intolerant and unkind and narrow to say that there's only one way to get into heaven?"

Not at all; there's only one way to do a lot of things in our world:

- There's only one way to add 2+2.
- There's only one way to land a jet plane on an aircraft carrier.
- There's only one way to launch the nuclear arsenal of the United States.

Do people get offended and accuse naval aviators or mathematicians or the person carrying the atomic football of being intolerant? Of course not!

So if there really is only one way to get to heaven, then there is nothing mean about God telling us so or intolerant about us as believers telling others what God has told us.

Objection #2: "Why would God be so unfair to people who don't believe in Jesus?"

In asking this question, we reveal a lack of biblical understanding regarding the true state of human beings in the eyes of an all-holy God.

Romans 5:12: "Therefore, just as through one man sin entered the world, and death through sin, and thus death spread to all men, because all sinned" (NKJV).

The Bible teaches that when Adam and Eve disobeyed God in the Garden of Eden, they brought a flaw upon the entire human race.

- A flaw the Bible calls our "sin nature." It's like a "defective gene" that every member of the human race inherits. And the result of this is that every human being is born "dead in trespasses and sins" (Ephesians 2:1 NKJV).

- The Bible says that every one of us is born spiritually dead: alienated from God, separated from God, and under God's fair and righteous judgment. This is why John 3:18 says, "He who does not believe is condemned already" (NKJV).
- Now, in His mercy, God made a way for us to escape this predicament through Jesus' atoning work on the cross for us. But if someone rejects God's way of mercy and ends up experiencing God's judgment, has God been unfair to that person? Of course not!

Recently, the price of bulk silver went up to its highest level in years. I have a bunch of bulk silver that I bought many years ago, but I did not make any money on it. The reason is that, when I purchased my silver in 1980, it was at $35 an ounce. In fact, I got so caught up in the silver frenzy going on back then that I emptied our entire savings account and bought silver with it!

In 1980, when I went into my local coin shop to make my historic silver purchase, there was a sign with huge letters by the cash register that read: **"All Sales Final—No Exceptions!"** And when I was checking out, the

Thomas (The Exclusivity of Jesus for Salvation)

owner pointed this sign out to me and said, "You see that sign, right? And you understand it, right?"

And I said, "Yes, sir, I do."

Within one week of my purchase, the bottom fell out of the silver market and prices dropped like a rock. I called the coin shop owner and explained to him what I had done and how I was in danger of losing my entire life savings. I begged him to please let me return the silver for the original price I'd paid for it.

He replied, "Didn't I ask you if you saw and understood the sign? I'm sorry, but it means what it says."

So I still have all that silver to this day. In fact, I would be happy to sell it to anyone reading this right now for exactly what I paid for it!

So here's the question: Was that coin shop owner "unfair" to me? The answer is no. He told me what the rules were and then he enforced the rules. I was *foolish*, but he was not *unfair*.

By the same token, God tells people over and over again in the Bible what the rules are: "No one comes to the Father except through me" (John 14:6 NKJV). "Nor is there salvation in any other" (Acts 4:12 NKJV).

And then God pleads with people to listen and pay attention and obey. But if people choose not to listen and obey, it is not about God being unfair—it's about people being foolish.

Objection #3: "What about people who have never heard about Jesus?"

Romans 1:20: "For since the creation of the world His invisible attributes are clearly seen, being understood by the things that are made, even His eternal power and Godhead, so that they are without excuse" (NKJV).

The Bible says there is enough about God revealed in creation and the natural world all around us that every human being alive should clearly understand that there is a mighty Creator God out there. We all should also understand that we should earnestly seek out this God, and that when we do this, God takes the responsibility to get us the specific information about Jesus we need to believe and be saved.

I can personally testify to the truth of this.

In the summer of 1965, I spent six weeks at Virginia Tech participating in the National Science Foundation summer seminar program for outstanding high school rising seniors from across the United States. In the afternoons, we worked on individual research projects, and in the mornings we all attended class together.

Thomas (The Exclusivity of Jesus for Salvation)

The subject of one of these classes was the human enzyme system. In that class, we learned that our bodies have thousands of enzymes that enable virtually every chemical reaction inside of us. And the most amazing thing we learned is that each of these enzymes only does its one job. If an enzyme is missing or defective, no other enzyme will take its place or do what it was designed to do. And it only takes one missing or defective enzyme out of thousands to make a person critically ill or terminal.

I remember learning this one morning and walking back to my dorm at lunchtime, pondering the impossibility of such an amazingly complex system being the result of chance or Darwinian evolution. When I got to the top of the stairs about to enter my dorm, standing there in the bright sunlight, I looked up into the heavens and said out loud: "There has got to be a God."

Although I knew nothing about this God, in keeping with Romans 1:20, natural creation had done its job inside me. It had brought me to the stark realization that there had to be an omnipotent Creator God. And, in God's perfect timing, six years later, God put Bob Eckhart, a street preacher, right in front of me on Franklin Street in Chapel Hill, North Carolina. He made sure I got all the information about Jesus that I needed so I could believe and be saved.

The point is that, if as a result of the natural revelation in creation, a person will humbly acknowledge in his or her heart that the omnipotent creator God, the Lord, will provide the rest of the information needed to complete the process of coming to Christ. And conversely, if a person refuses to humbly acknowledge the existence of this God, in spite of the overwhelming nature of the evidence, He holds that person "without excuse."

Objection #4: "Let's say someone looks around at creation and acknowledges that there is a God—but that person chooses to pursue Him through Buddhism or Islam or Shintoism or Taoism or Judaism or whatever. Can't God just credit such people with the blood of Jesus even if they don't realize He's doing this or take them to heaven anyway?"

God "can" do anything, but He says in the Bible that He "won't" do this.

Romans 10:9: "If you confess with your mouth the Lord Jesus and believe in your heart that God has raised Him from the dead, you will be saved" (NKJV).

The key point here is that to "confess with your mouth the Lord Jesus and believe in your heart that God

Thomas (The Exclusivity of Jesus for Salvation)

has raised Him from the dead" necessitates that you hear the gospel message of the Bible and have decided to willingly, knowingly, and factually to embrace it.

This is why Romans 10:17 says, "So then faith [in Jesus that brings us eternal life and heaven] comes by hearing, and hearing by the word of God [the Bible]" (NKJV).

The most sincere Muslim, Jew, Buddist, Hindu, Scientologist, Confuscian, Shintoist, Christian Scientist, atheist, or secular American do-gooder—until that person *hears* the cognitive facts about Jesus from the Bible (His virgin birth, deity, sinless life, death on the cross, blood payment for our sins, and resurrection from the dead)—and believes it—that person is lost!

This is what the Bible teaches without hesitation, without reservation, and without equivocation.

In conclusion, as believers in Christ, we must realize that apart from faith in Jesus, all the people we encounter—every day, everywhere—are separated from God, are under God's judgment for sin, and are headed for disaster when they enter eternity.

We must realize that the only hope these people have is for us as believers to open our mouths and lovingly share with them the cognitive facts of the Bible about Jesus and His plan for salvation.

But the only way you and I are ever going to be boldly vocal like this is if we believe that, outside of faith in Jesus, all people are utterly, totally, and hopelessly lost in hell for all eternity.

If you are a believer in Jesus, I hope I've been able to put this issue to rest in your heart today, once and for all.

And I hope you will walk away from this chapter taking seriously the Apostle Paul's words to Timothy (2 Timothy 1:8): "Therefore do not be ashamed of the testimony of our Lord" (NKJV). In other words, be a missionary every day!

Finally, if you are reading this and have never embraced Jesus and what He did on the cross for you as your one and only hope of possessing eternal life and entering heaven, then I would like to offer the opportunity to do that right now.

Please pray this prayer with me with all the sincerity in your heart:

> Lord Jesus, today I come to humble myself before You and to confess that I am a sinner who is alienated and separated from You because of my sin.

Thomas (The Exclusivity of Jesus for Salvation)

Today, I want to repent of my sinfulness and turn from it to You. Today, I agree to reject all other remedies I have trusted to have my sins forgiven and to get into heaven—my good works, my religious activity, my trying to be a good person. And today, I agree to rely on Your work on the cross for me—shedding Your blood to pay for my sins in the sight of an all-holy God—as my one and only plan for attaining eternal life and entry into heaven. Today, I surrender my life to You as my Lord and Savior from the penalty of all my sins. In Jesus' name I pray, Amen!

www.ingramcontent.com/pod-product-compliance
Lightning Source LLC
Chambersburg PA
CBHW022111090426
42743CB00008B/809